D0770475

With Wings As Eagles

BY JOHN RANDOLPH PRICE

Books

*The Abundance Book
Angel Energy
The Angels Within Us
*Empowerment
*The Planetary Commission
*Practical Spirituality
*A Spiritual Philosophy for the New World
*The Superbeings
*With Wings As Eagles

Selected Audiocassettes

*Flight of the Eagle
*The 40-Day Prosperity Plan
*Global Mind Link/World Healing Meditation
The Hidden Splendor
The Incredible Power of Love
*A Journey Into the Fourth Dimension
*The Manifestation Process
The Mind of One Vibration
*Prayer, Principles & Power
The Twenty-Two Angels of the Kingdom

Items with asterisks can be ordered through Hay House:
800-654-4126 • 800-650-5115 (fax)

Please visit the Hay House Website at:
http://www.hayhouse.com

With Wings As Eagles

Discovering the Master Teacher in the Secret School Within

John Randolph Price

HAY HOUSE

Hay House, Inc.
Carlsbad, CA

Hay House, Inc.
Carlsbad, CA
Copyright © 1987 by John Randolph Price
Revised Edition Copyright © 1997

Published and distributed in the United States by:
Hay House, Inc., P.O. Box 5100, Carlsbad, CA 92018-5100
(800) 654-5126 • (800) 650-5115 (fax)

This book was originally published by Quartus Books, Boerne, Texas, in 1987.

All rights reserved. No part of this book may be reproduced by any mechanical, photographic, or electronic process, or in the form of a phonographic recording, nor may it be stored in a retrieval system, transmitted, or otherwise be copied for public or private use—other than for "fair use" as brief quotations embodied in articles and reviews without prior written permission of the publisher.

Library of Congress Cataloging-in-Publication Data

Price, John Randolph.
    With wings as eagles : discovering the master teacher in the
secret school within / John Randolph Price.
        p.   cm.
    Originally published: Austin, Tex. : Quartus Books, 1987.
    ISBN: 1-56170-359-1 (trade paper)
    1. Spiritual life--Miscellanea. I. Title.
BF1999.P723 1996
299'.93--dc21   96-46850
                                                        CIP

ISBN 1-56170-359-1

00 99 98 97   4 3 2 1

First Printing, Hay House Edition, February 1997

Printed in the United States of America

This book is dedicated to the Eagles on Earth and beyond, those mighty Souls of Light who have spread their wings and have commenced the Journey Home to the Secret Place on the Mountain, the very Kingdom of God.

CONTENTS

Introduction

Since 1981, the major points I have tried to make in the writing of my spiritual-metaphysical books have been:

1. My conviction that the members of the fourth kingdom (humanity) are divine beings who descended into the third-dimensional plane, lost their spiritual consciousness, and have since been seeking their true Identity.

2. The fact that a growing number of "humans" have attained cosmic consciousness and are now living on Planet Earth with dominion over the physical world. These are the men and women who have totally mastered the physical, emotional, and mental bodies and have risen to a new frequency of consciousness where all effects of the phenomenal world reflect the Truth within. They are living with financial independence, whole and well bodies, creative success, and ideal relationships. And what one can do, all can do.

3. There are many paths to the Mountaintop and no exclusive route. We are all moving as one toward the reawakening, regardless of our religious indoctrination—and the only Leader is the Master within.

4. The belief that peace on earth can become a reality, and the inner knowingness that the planet will be harmonized when a sufficient number of people change their consciousness to a vibration of love, forgiveness, and understanding. This led to the plan for the global mind-link in 1986 and the planetary affirmation of peace and love to achieve a critical mass of spiritual consciousness.

Overall, my objective has been to help people transform their personal lives through the renewing of their minds, to paraphrase St. Paul, and to restore this world to sanity by affecting a major change in the collective consciousness. It is to seek and affirm the innate divinity of all, and through prayer and meditation to realize the Master within, the Spirit of God who is "above all, through all, and in all"—with the freedom to express the highest that is in each one of us.

To achieve this freedom, we must have peace in our minds, love in our hearts, and forgiveness in our souls. Only then will understanding become the common bond of the planetary family. In this book, you will find that peace—a sense of serenity that comes from knowing the dynamic Reality within that is constantly in expression as all that is good, true, and beautiful in life. You will discover the love that created you in the beginning and sustains you moment by moment, enabling you to be a radiating center of unconditional love to all those you encounter. Complete forgiveness will come as the awareness grows that there is nothing to forgive—that all is consciousness in action reflecting back to us what we most need to learn about ourselves. And then one day, perhaps unexpectedly, we will awaken from a deep sleep, and a new understanding dawns. We see the world differently because we have changed our minds from the old belief system of the self-created ego to the pure knowing of Divine Consciousness. Our world then reflects true Cause, the very Goodwill of God, and harmony becomes the law of being.

It is time.

— John Randolph Price

Foreword

Listen. The time is now. Hear the sounds of freedom. No longer must you walk in the hot sands of a life tormented by fear and desperation. Standing before you is the way out of the wilderness of futility and despair. It is the way of the eagle. I say to you this day: Look to the eagle. To those who are lost, *the eagle shall spreadeth her wings, taketh them, beareth them on her wings.*[1] And you shall find the Mountain, the Secret Place shall be opened, and the Light shall greet you saying, *I bare you on eagles wings, and brought you unto myself.*[2]

What is the eagle? The eagle is the inner yearning to escape from bondage, the ancient memory of the Divine Self, the resolve to break the chains of humanhood and return to Christhood. The eagle is courage and tenacity, vision and power, the energy within each soul that refuses to be bound, the consciousness that knows only freedom.

Listen for the eagle and you will hear the call to commence the Journey Home. The instruction is so simple, yet the rewards so great: *They that wait upon the Lord shall renew their strength; they shall mount up with wings as eagles; they shall run, and not be weary; and they shall walk, and not faint.*[3]

To wait upon the Lord has a double meaning, or as the

Ancients say, a twin-flame decree.

It is to *stand still and see the salvation of the Lord* [4] — a resting in expectation of the mighty works of Omnipotence to transform all appearances and seeing with awe and wonder *the victory that overcometh the world.* [5]

It is to commit yourself without reservation to the service of the Inner Master — not a sentence of servitude, but a joyful and loving dedication to serve the Holy High Self with the fullness of your being.

Those who wait upon the Living Christ within shall indeed be strong. *Their youth is renewed like the eagle's,* [6] and they shall rise from their sickbeds and stand forth with vigor and power, knowing only the Life Force of Wholeness. They shall be lifted above deprivation and scarcity to soar into the limitless substance of abundance. They shall be protected under the shadow of the Almighty, and no evil shall befall them. They will be set on high, on a rock, above all sorrow and anguish. And their hearts shall be opened to love, a love so great, so unconditional, that it will attract to them heaven's boundless measure of adoration.

Those who give up self for the Holy Self shall find the Way; they shall have wings as eagles, and into the heavens they shall fly, a flight of joy and gladness taking them to the Secret Place on the Mountain, the very Kingdom of God. And there, they shall run, and not be weary; and they shall walk, and not faint.

The Dawn approaches. The Kingdom awaits. It is now time for the Gathering of Eagles in preparation for flight.

1. Duet. 32:11.
2. Ex. 19:4.
3. Is. 40:31.
4. Ex. 14:13.
5. 1 John 5:4.
6. Ps. 103:5.

1

The School
and The Teacher

A secret school of higher learning exists in the world today. It is secret by reason that it is hidden from all but those who are dedicated to rediscovering and realizing their divinity. I call it *The School of Truth* because it represents the highest wisdom of the collective mind of man. In its essential character, it can be identified as the *Spiritual Consciousness* of humanity—the divine understanding of untold numbers of men and women who have walked on this planet to seek and discover the Holy Self within.

You will find students and graduates of the School throughout the pages of world history—in the esoteric societies of ancient Egypt, Persia, and Greece; as Qabbalah initiates; among the Hindu and Buddhist Mystics and the Gnostics of early Christianity; in the inner circle of Mohammad and the initiates in the Arabian Mysteries; as the alchemists of the Middle Ages; the soldier mystics of the Knights Templar; in the roots of the Rosicrucian Order; in the tradition of Freemasonry; among the Transcendentalists of the 1800's, and the Esotericists and New Thinkers of the Twentieth Century.

Their common goal is the spiritual awakening of humanity. Their emblem is the eagle—for aeons the symbol of initiation into mastery.

The wisdom of the Consciousness of Truth may be briefly

1

summarized thusly: God is Supreme Being, the *IS*, the All-In-All, Unmanifest and Manifest. The *IS* ideates the *I AM*, the Son, The Universal Spirit, the omnipresent God-Man, the Divine Self Who individualizes as Centers of Consciousness for *Self*-awareness. As Expressions of the Spirit of God, these Holy Ones experienced the fullness of creation, only in time to slip into the dream of mortality and lose the awareness of individual divinity. Through the teachings of the Elders of the race, they began the journey home... toward at-one-ment and reunion with the Eternal One within, the true Self. The initiates who resurrect the Self within are called Masters. Mastery is achieved through consecration to the service of humanity, an understanding of the laws of Nature, the knowledge of form as the symbol of the activity of God behind the form, the glorification of the Divine Self within... leading ultimately to the illumination of the mind, transmutation of the emotions, and regeneration of the body. At the moment of the Awakening, the authority of the Spiritual Self is released, with the man, the woman, possessing the power of dominion over every limitation in the physical world.[1]

The consciousness of Truth in the invisible world has created a Hall of Wisdom on the inner plane — an Arena of Energy that hovers over the physical world and forms an etheric School — which can also be described as *an atmosphere conducive to*

---

1. While belief in God Immanent and the unity of all life may be considered purely "New Age" philosophy to some, it must be remembered that it is preliterary and has served as the foundation for the advances in literature, art, the sciences, medicine, and mathematics. Throughout history, the Truth of the divinity of man has been the guiding Light for the builders of civilization. Just look at the contributions made by Pythagoras, Socrates, Plato, Aristotle, Hypatia, Roger Bacon, Dante, Paracelsus, Leonardo da Vinci, Francis Bacon, Galileo, Robert Fludd, Descartes, Spinoza, Robert Boyle, Issac Newton, Swedenborg, Alexander Pope, Benjamin Franklin, Van Goethe, Coleridge, Thomas Carlyle, Victor Hugo, Emerson, Theodore Parker, Tennyson, Robert Browning, Thoreau, Nathaniel Hawthorne, Walt Whitman, Oliver Wendell Holmes, Gandi, Jung, Claude Debussy, William James — to name only a few "New Agers" of their day — all knowers of the Oneness of God and Man.

learning. Men and women on Earth who are drawn to the serious study of Truth are overshadowed by this Energy and resonate to its vibration.

This energy, which works with the soul aspect of man, serves to provide a Force Field to accelerate the learning process. Through its radiation, it supports the student in preserving the spiritual commitment—regardless of the obstacles encountered. It also functions as a magnetic field to separate through non-affinity the Seekers of the Word and the laggards who refuse the Path of Sonship. There is no judgement or condemnation involved in the "separation"...it simply means that Truth Students will be attracted to each other through particular vibrations in consciousness, thus forming groups of like minds to stimulate awakening—*while continuing to develop and maintain unconditional love toward all people, regardless of their belief system.*

In addition, this Energy Field amplifies the telepathic work of Spiritual Guides in communicating with those in the physical world, and provides a spiritual Environment for "classes" on the inner plane. The many dreams you have had of contact with Souls in the higher realm and the instructions received— represent etheric plane activity at the School while asleep. Finally, with the conscious cooperation of the student through dedication to meditation and spiritual living, the Energy will stimulate the Realization Process and assist in the removal of the memory seal.

The Spiritual Consciousness of the Awakened Ones constitutes the School of Truth, and Seekers of Truth in both non-physical and physical form make up the student body. Regarding the latter group, one common denominator among the *dedicated* ones seems to be discernment in the area of "casting pearls"—a reluctance to dissipate spiritual energy by engaging in proselytism. The result of this privateness has led, to some extent, to the creation of an image akin to a secret society. Perhaps C.S. Lewis was talking about such people when he wrote in *Mere Christianity:*

> "Every now and then one meets them. Their very
> voices and faces are different from ours; stronger,

quieter, happier, more radiant. They begin where
most of us leave off. When you have recognized one
of them, you will recognize the next one much more
easily. And I strongly suspect that they recognize
each other immediately and infallibly, across every
barrier of color, sex, class, age and even of creeds. In
that way, to become holy is rather like joining a
secret society."

You and countless others before you have already joined the
secret society. Through your dedication to spiritual principles,
you have enrolled in the School to find your Holiness, and one
day you will graduate...with a Masters Degree. The timing is
up to you, but know this: Every Awakened Soul in the spiritual
realm is offering his/her Energy to serve as the "Institution" for
your higher learning.

My purpose in bringing the School to your attention is to
establish the *fact* that you are never alone on your quest. Living
Souls of Light have formed a sacred Environment for you, and
are inviting you to partake of its vibrations. Pause for a
moment, close your eyes, and *feel* the Energy of the Awakened
Ones enfold you. Sense the Consciousness of Wisdom all
around you. Open your heart to the Love of this Great Council
of Souls.

To acknowledge their Presence does not mean to desert the
Master Teacher within and the search for your own Truth. Quite
the contrary. They are here to help you find *The Teacher*—and
to hold you secure in their glorious Circle of Love wherever you
are, wherever you go. The Energy of the Great Ones is influenc-
ing you even now with the truth that *you* are an integral part of
the grandest movement since the beginning...a shifting of the
entire consciousness of the human race toward Christhood.

The classes have begun. The Teacher is waiting.

The Teacher

At a point in time on our spiritual journey, Jan and I were
told by an Awakened One, "...my Truth is *my* Truth, not
yours. You must find your own Truth."

4

I didn't understand this comment at first, but it later dawned on me that he was right, because Truth must be realized individually. It must be realized by you, otherwise it is not your Truth. Only *your* Truth is expressed in your life, not anyone else's. How do you find your Truth? By seeking and finding The Teacher within. You see, The Teacher and the Truth are one, and once you have The Teacher, you have the Truth.

The search for The Teacher, however, may lead us up a few blind alleys if we're not careful. Sometimes we think we've found the Master Light, only to find upon closer inspection that it is only a dim substitute. Let me give you a few examples.

As we begin to work with metaphysical principles, the initial opening in consciousness may release the "wish life" from the subconscious. As these desires are thrown on the screen of mind, we may mistakenly "hear" them as instructions from God. Isn't it wonderful that God tells us to do just what we think we'd like to do? But before we run off in all directions seeking the dream, our intuition tells us to slow down, be still, and wait. Some of us listened. Many of us didn't. Those who did soon understood that a desire is not always from the Father—that fantasies may also be avenues of escape that we have created to break free of responsibilities. And we continued on the inner journey.

However, those of us who didn't heed the caution light took off for new horizons, and while we may have felt liberated in the beginning, we soon found that our consciousness went with us on the new adventure. Oh my. Those same problems we were running from were there, too—along with another set of needs to be fulfilled. So we back-tracked and started over again.

After we move through the wish-life stage, we seem to practice more discipline and devotion in our spiritual work. This tighter focus results in flashes of remembrances of spiritual ideas buried deeply in our memory banks. When these memory cells relating to our true Identity are first aroused, the energy of spiritual attunement from countless past lives begins to rise in the subjective chamber. As these spiritual thoughts and ideas move into the conscious mind, they may be considered "new" to the person's present state of consciousness, and therefore attributed to channeled messages from the higher spiritual realm, or from the Higher Self within. What we must understand at this juncture is that many of us have been on the spiritual path for numerous incarnations and we have built up quite a reservoir of recollection energy—much of it from previous religious studies and the reading of spiritual materials. So what we're actually doing here is reading our personal Akashic Records—those that pertain to our spiritual work. Some people have given this energy the name of a biblical figure and have gone public with the "new" revelations. This is not to say that the information is not valuable. Much of it is helpful in raising consciousness and turning people toward the Light within. But the messages do not represent the fullness of the One Who is to come through the *Realization Experience* in this incarnation. We cannot live on yesterday's manna, no matter how high and mighty we may have been in an earlier life.

As we continue the "reading" of our recollection energy, we'll move into a level of consciousness where we become aware (the first step in the realization process) that there actually *is* a Presence within, a Higher Mind, a Power that is greater than anything in the outer world. Through this awareness, something deep within us is stirred. It is the ancient memory of our divinity—not just mental impressions of a former spiritual journey. And even though it is only a tiny flicker of light at first, the remembrance causes the energy to whirl around that Divine Idea, and like a whirlpool, it draws to it the energy of Truth from the Higher Realm. This transformation is slow and weak at first, but as we continue with the correct use of meditation, the awareness grows stronger in our conscious mind, leading to greater understanding on the subjective level.

New channels of communication now begin to open and contact with our spiritual guides is made. This contact is usually via energy impulses, intuitive promptings, and impressions in the mind. As I have written in *Practical Spirituality*, our guides work with us through energy transmissions stepped down to the vibration where we are at the time. Their role is to help us transmute our lower nature, inspire us to action in the service of others, alert us to unforeseen dangers, and herald the coming of the

One within.

As the whirling motion of the energy continues to grow more powerful, a passage or channel for Spirit is finally cleared. . . and the Voice speaks. Again, in the early stages it may only be an intuitive impulse because we are not yet completely at home with the language of Spirit, but we *feel* the difference and know with all our heart that the prompting is from on High. Soon we become familiar with the language, and the Voice of The Teacher is heard in consciousness.

Who is this Teacher? It is the Spirit of God within us — our Christ Self functioning as our very own *consciousness* through the process of realization. A I point out in another chapter, there are *degrees* of realization, so to minimize misinterpretation at the beginning of the process, Spirit releases the recollection energy from the subconscious relating to our highest spiritual Truth in previous incarnations. Since this knowledge is from our own memory banks, we will accept it with little distortion. Then as the vibration of our energy field grows stronger, the Christ Spirit can speak, and as the realization of the Presence deepens, the Voice is heard with greater and greater clarity.

It is interesting that as we move into the Energy of Spirit, we also find it possible to receive transmissions from the Awakened Ones in the higher spiritual realm — those who may well be in a higher state of consciousness than our guides. It is as though the inner Self sometimes allows meaningful communications from initiates to come through its consciousness and voice. This is another source of channeling based on energy correspondence, i.e. initiate to initiate according to the level of initiation taken by both parties.

There may also be an overshadowing of a high Master when an individual's motives are pure and his/her vibration is felt in the higher realm. My understanding of this was enhanced when I asked Spirit — "Why is there a need for a Spiritual Hierarchy or other Teachers? You are the Spirit of Truth. . . why do we need anyone else?" The answer: *"A Master Teacher is one who has brought the lower mind into the higher realm of Soul and dropped the personality or ego, but the experience of lower plane existence remains a part of his consciousness. Thus there is a basis for the teachings, and those on the lower plane may benefit from the blend of earth experience and the divine wisdom of the Christ Consciousness."*

Understand that making contact with a Master on a higher plane must not be our primary objective. That is simply a by-product of the realization process. Since the period of research involved in the writing of *The Superbeings*, I have cautioned people about getting caught up in the glamour of being a devotee of some ascended Master Soul, saying that this directs the spiritual focus away from Self and can delay the individual's Awakening. Just seek the Kingdom *first*, and any other transmissions needed for your growth will be "added."

You may wonder about people who have not been serious Truth students but who have had extraordinary experiences in the form of psychic visions of a spiritual nature, communications from the higher plane via automatic writing, or the sudden appearance of a Master in the kitchen. Regardless of the degree of spiritual preparation that preceded these experiences, the time was obviously right for those particular individuals involved—which shows us that we cannot judge where another person is in consciousness.

Regarding physical (unascended) teachers who have built spiritual organizations around their writings, some may be very helpful in pointing you in the direction of the Light and in opening consciousness to receive the Truth, but to blindly follow a guru is to desert the Who of You—and to devote your life to another person's mandatory initiation ritual and steps to enlightenment is folly. No one in the world knows you better than your Christ Self. Only The Teacher within knows where you are in consciousness and what steps must be taken for your ultimate Christing. Only when you know *your* Teacher of Truth will you be free to fly out of the tomb of mortality.

Schoolbooks and Lessons.

To have a School and a Teacher implies books and lessons. In this case, Spirit will provide the lessons and *you* will write the book. It will be *your* book based on your receptivity to Spirit, so I ask you to begin now to channel the Teachings of your Master within. Through contemplative meditation on the Presence you'll stir up the memory cells, giving you the opportunity to review your reservoir of recollection energy. Let it flow and write it down. Then start interpreting those higher impulses and intuitive promptings that are sure to come. Listen and record them daily.

If there are only feelings and symbols at first, ask yourself, "What do I intuitively feel that Spirit is saying to me?" — and write what comes into your mind. Meditate, listen, write. Meditate, listen, write. Or if you work better with a cassette recorder, meditate, listen, and speak what's coming through — then write the messages in your spiritual journal later.

The "lessons" that will fill your journal will deal with ways to deepen the realization of the Presence, how to co-create with Spirit to move beyond a challenge, ideas to make your spiritual work more effective, weaknesses in consciousness that must be strengthened, glimpses of the future, dream interpretations, and on and on. And be prepared to also receive transmissions from the Evolved Ones on a wide range of topics.

I have found it helpful to go into a period of deep, relaxed meditation, and speak the following: "Beloved Christ within, the Living God of my being, I humbly invite you to think through me now. I won't try to stop my own thinking, nor will I try to think specific thoughts. I'll simply let go and let You speak into my mind." And then affirm: "The Christ Presence is now using my mind to think, and I am totally receptive to the Word."

Usually I will speak this statement aloud three times, and then silently three times, which shifts my consciousness into the listening mode. As the thoughts begin to come through, they are transcribed by pen on paper, or by typewriter — and then I spend time studying and meditating on the lessons for deeper realizations of truth.

Another method of tuning into the Higher Consciousness is to meditate for a time, then while you are still in that deeply relaxed but alert state, let your imagination take you into the forest or to a mountain. There, meet someone who in your mind represents divine wisdom and understanding. Perhaps it's a kindly old man with white hair who beckons you to come sit beside him. Greet this image with great honor and respect, and look into his eyes immediately. You may ask his name if you like, and he will surely respond. When you feel comfortable with your friend, begin to ask your questions. Move into a relaxed give-and-take dialogue, as if in an informal interview with a Master Soul.

In *Practical Spirituality* I wrote about my imaginary meeting on the cliff with Asher. This wise old man represented (to me) the Master Energy of my Higher Self giving me a view of the world and a look at the future. I've been asked if this was a case of overshadowing by an evolved one or actually the voice of Self. The transmission came into my consciousness on the frequency of the inner Teacher, so whether it was the Spirit of JRP or a Brother who called himself Asher is not important. You see, when we tap into the vibration of the Superconsciousness, we are on the *Frequency of Oneness*. And it is on this Frequency that we can be in tune with Spirit within *and* the Active Intelligence of the Awakened Ones—yet the transmission comes from or through the voice of The Teacher within. If you are writing the messages as they come through, you can sometimes detect a different rhythm in the sentence structure and changes in the communication style. If that arouses your curiosity, ask for identification. The response will usually be the designation that you are most comfortable with in referring to your Higher Self, or a name which corresponds to the Mind Energy communicating with you at the time.

Again, the messages (lessons) will come through the channel of your Higher Consciousness, and the Frequency of Oneness will assure receptivity to Universal Inspiration, the Spirit expressing in all. This is why I like to refer to *Spirit* as the Source of all the messages I receive.

The first intuitive message that I attributed to Spirit came forth in 1967, and ten years later I heard the first audible words. During those years and continuing to this day I've received enough messages to fill several books. In fact, my books are, for the most part, the result of communications from within—colored of course by my own particular energy and conditioned to the degree of my realization of Truth. A few examples follow in the next two chapters—edited to provide a sense of continuity.

We will start with a sample of my lessons, but understand that the primary reason for sharing this material with you is to open your mind and heart and stimulate you to find the Divine Schoolhouse...to stir you to formally enroll in the exciting Course of Soul Evolution...and to inspire you to produce your own textbook based on the lessons received from the Master You.

Your book will be the most meaningful one you've ever read because it will be the one written specifically for *you*.

2

The Lessons — Part I

You say that you have faith in God, that you believe in God, that your trust God. But I ask you, how can you believe in God and profess faith and trust if you do not know *me*? Yes, I am closer than your very breath, but what meaning does that have for you?

If you were attempting to be friendly to a new neighbor, or were establishing a relationship with an acquaintance, would you not take the time to get to *know* the individual? Your first consideration would be one of courtesy, kindness and respect. If the neighbor or the acquaintance knocked at your door, your response would be to welcome the person and express hospitality. You would talk, share, and listen together. Yet when I knock at the door of your consciousness, ready to provide you with the Word and the Way, I am usually ignored.

You do not talk to me, nor do you listen to me. It is as if I did not exist. . . until there is a problem. Can you not understand that I am alive, that I live, that I am a living being? I think, I see, I speak, I listen, I know, I love. Am I not worthy to be acknowledged, at least in the measure of a neighbor or an acquaintance? Am I not at least as important as your troubles? Then why do you think more about your troubles than you do of me?

You cannot say that you have not had the benefit of my presence, because I know that you have felt the feeling of love in your heart. You cannot say that you have not seen me, because I appear as Light to the inner eye and an overshadowing presence to your mind. You cannot say that you have not heard me, for I am forever speaking through your intuition and whispering thoughts into your mind.

Who am I? What is there in a name, a word, or a title? I wear many faces. Some call me the Christ. To others I am God. I am also referred to as the Father, the Son, the Holy Spirit, the Monad, Atma, Buddi, Higher Mind, Soul, Self. Consciously, I am all of these, depending on my vibrational frequency. Simply said, I am your higher, finer, lighter Energy. I am all that you once were and can be again. I am the Purity of you, the Reality of you, the Life of you, the Essence of you, the Love of you, the Person of you.

To the personality of the lower self, I am a friend, guide, teacher, perfector of concerns, freer of burdens, healer of ills, filler of lacks, and harmonizer of conditions. Even more, I am the cause, creator, source—and the effect, the creation, the result. Understand this.

Where am I? I am around, in, and through you. You live, move and have your being in me, and I in you. When you sit, I sit with you. When you walk, I walk with you. I am where you are—eternally.

It is dawning on you now, as you think of the who and the where of me, that I am You—the You not caught in the web of the illusion, the You of a higher dimension. Do you see me? I exist simultaneously in all dimensions, all planes, all frequencies and vibrations. I am pure Light, yet my radiance dims on the lower plane of consciousness. I am the Cosmic Fire, yet my flame is but a flicker in the depths of mortal mind. I am the Music of the Spheres, yet my harmony rings unmelodious in the world of materiality.

Now do you see me? Do you see *You*? There is but One . . . there is no "we" . . . there is only I. From the highest of the above to the lowest of the below, there is only I.

When I say *talk to me, listen to me,* the "me" is not some-thing separate from you. It is the inner you, the deeper you, the higher you, the holy you. Can you not talk to your Self, listen to

14

your Self, love your Self?

There is much talk about Masters. Why do you seek one outside of yourself when you have the Master Energy of the universe within you? Why do you seek the opinions and beliefs of others when all Truth is yours? No other individual, whether visible or invisible, can affect a realization of Truth within your consciousness. No Teacher, in physical or nonphysical form, can know the Truth for you with any lasting effect. It is only when you know and express *your* Truth that you are free. I am your Truth. Know me and be free.

⋄ ⋄ ⋄

You have heard that love is the fulfilling of the law. It is also the way of attaining the Experience. Understand that I am the pure essence of love, and my love for you is my eternal Gift to you. As you receive my love and *accept it,* I become real to you. The shadows flee, the old is made new, and your life is transformed according to the level of the realization. To receive this Gift, you must reach deeply within for it, and it must be your love that reaches out *to* me and *for* me. This is the meaning of "Give and you shall receive." You must first open the channel to receive. The Gift for you is love. To receive the Gift of Love, you must give love. Think of two hands reaching out to touch. This is symbolic of our rays of love coming together. At the moment of contact, I am realized. Now do you see why the greatest commandment is to love me? To love me is to make the connection. To make the connection is to realize my presence. *Love unceasingly!*

⋄ ⋄ ⋄

Dismiss all thoughts of right and wrong, for in truth, man has done neither. Every action you have ever taken was as a child running home in the darkness of night. If you stumbled, it was because you could not see. If you fell, it was your loss of balance. Why call it right or wrong? Set a clock to a certain time and wind it up. The mechanism is running, the clock is ticking. Unless the hands are changed, the clock will proceed on a definite course. The consciousness of man is like the clock. Unless it is changed, it will continue as is. Once set, it is *in action,* and everything it feels, thinks, says or does is dictated by its beliefs. Are they right? Are they wrong? That is not the point. The point is, man cannot act contrary to his consciousness. He cannot express any differently than he is in consciousness. Understand this and forgiveness toward all will not be difficult.

✧ ✧ ✧

Consider a challenge as a choice, a choice made by you to reinforce your I AM — to realize that I AM the answer, the solution. *I* am the I AM. I am Omnipotence and nothing can stand against me, and remember that I am you. This You that I AM is a present help in every difficulty, seeking only to move through your consciousness and touch the unreal appearance — and it is no more. In its place is the reality of harmony. Can you not trust me? Will you not let *me* be responsible for that which concerns you? You chose the challenge to prove me, yet when the test appeared, you forgot me. You staged the performance and cast me as the hero, as the deliverer and producer of miracles, yet when the play began I was left out of the script — replaced by you and your mortal sense of stress and strain. Without me, the challenge cannot be met. . . it can only be replaced with another challenge. With me, only the good is triumphant. I AM always victorious in every situation. Trust me!

✧ ✧ ✧

You cannot possess health anymore than you can possess illness, for you can only have that which I AM. I am neither health nor illness. I am perfection, therefore, the part of myself that you are is perfect. If you will meditate on your oneness with me and become aware of me as the purity of your being, you will be free of the idea of imperfection. Unless it is karmic illness chosen for purification, in which case your soul will refuse the illumination, my Light will move through your awareness and remove the shadow of the illness. No, the illness is not replaced with health. The Light does not reveal a form of disease and heal it. It simply reveals the *absence* of any imperfection.

Too much emphasis has been placed on mental causes of disease, what may be called wrong thinking. While it is true that energy follows thought, the primary process of disease are beliefs born and nurtured in the emotional nature through a trend of inharmonious living. You may say that whenever energy is blocked, and circulation through the centers is inhibited by a disposition toward conflict, dissension, hostility— pockets of darkness form in the physical system affecting the glands and leading to disease. While there is no incurable disease, it will remain in or near the body until the purification is complete, or as long as the lower nature is out of control, and until the emotional system is transmuted. If you would have wholeness, *be* whole in living. (And) through meditation on the Christ *within,* the lower faculties begin to glorify the Lord and become receptive to the Light. Where there is Light, there is no darkness, no imperfection.

·◇· ·◇· ·◇·

There is a Fountain of Love within you, and from it flows the fulfillment of all you could desire, the light substance to bring every form into visibility. The Fountain is never in disrepair... its operation is eternally perfect and its power source is my love for you, a love so great that it is beyond your comprehension. The flow from the Fountain is endless and bountiful. Will you not stand in the stream with me now and eradicate all appearances of lack in your life? Come to me...come within and feel the rushing waters of infinite supply. Indeed your cup runneth over. There is no emptiness in my universe, no shortages, no limitations. All is forever filled full. Can you understand that I am the Fountain, the Flow, and the Fulfillment? Can you now interpret this as the Source, the Cause, and the Effect?

Now consider this, for it is very important. There is something between me and your phenomenal world. It is your consciousness. Your world mirrors that which is closest to it, therefore your world is reflecting *your* consciousness. If you would have your world reflect *my* nature of loving sufficiency, I must be brought into your consciousness—even to the outer rim, so to speak. There, I stand before your world and the Truth is revealed. No good thing is then withheld from you. But you must not direct or prescribe the way. I am the way. Leave it in my hands. Be as a little child in joyful anticipation, keeping your thoughts on me, caring not and trusting me, fearing not and loving me. I am the Way!

✧ ✧ ✧

Questions regarding the temptations of Jesus and His role as a Wayshower.

Do not live only for that which is made manifest. Enjoy all, but *live* for that which is omnipresent, the invisible essence of all that is. Behind the form is energy...the energy is from the Word...the Word is the force of my Knowing. Contemplate my Knowing and you will live by my Word in wholeness.

You cannot tempt me. The correct word in the second temptation is *test*, and it is not the Lord who shall be tested, but your consciousness of the Lord indwelling. You would not test a broken leg to see if it is healed by jumping from the roof, yet many attempt to verify their level of spiritual consciousness through premature action. Have you not cast yourself into uncertain situations, thinking you were divinely protected and under divine guidance, only to find that you were not ready for the risks taken? If you wish to test, or measure, your consciousness of God, behold your manifest life. Then, when it is time to leap into new waters, do so from the prompting of Spirit, not from the pushing of ego.

Do not let personality deceive you, for it seeks the glamour of power. It would tell you that the glory of the world is yours, and that the dark way of attainment is necessary to achieve the waiting treasures. By "dark" I am referring to means that are contrary to the highest good of all, a compromising of integrity, a judgement that sees those standing in the way as vulnerable to reaping what they have sown — thus justifying unprincipled actions, and a selfishness that seeks only to master. Know this: a master of the world is a servant of the world. Seek only to serve, first the Christ of your being, and then those who continue to sleep. In service you will find God. In service to Spirit, invisible and visible, the ego will be controlled and the angels will minister unto you.

There has been much contemplation of Jesus in your mind. There are two reasons for this. One, you are seeking a personal Truth concerning the Master to register in your body of convictions. Two, you seek to reconcile the seeming conflicts in philosophy and religion as to Jesus' role and status. Let us explore these ideas.

Jesus identified his mission at the beginning of his ministry: to change hearts and reveal the kingdom. He taught that the heart, or feeling nature, was the predetermining aspect of life, the transformer of energy into experience. The collective experience of humanity was one of great travail projecting from the emotions of fear, depravity and intolerance. If allowed to continue, it is likely that the evolution of man would have slowed to such an extent that "civilization" today would be entering that period of time called the Middle Ages. There was also the possibility of humanity being reduced to an even more primitive state than existed at the time. Knowing this, Jesus reintroduced the power of love by first releasing its energy into the world's mental currents. The effect was a greater receptivity to his teachings of Light.

Jesus established himself as the Ideal, as the World Light, then carefully transferred this recognition to all members of the human family by identifying each as the Light of the world—not to hide but to share as a sign of Sonship. Once the identification of divinity was confirmed, the love vibration was amplified in the emotions through the unconditional aspect of detachment, as taught in the secret of human relations: transmute anger, banish contempt, recognize the immaculate image of all, concur with your opponent, resist not, make peace with your brother, forgive all, and love your enemies. Jesus emphasized the naturalness of these practices by adding the admonition to be perfect, again associating man with his Creator.

With the lifting of man to his rightful status, if only through an intuitive recollection of his true rank, it was now time to kindle the remembrance of the kingdom. The kingdom, which is the Father's pleasure to give, is the realization of God. It is the consciousness of God's present Knowingness of every need and

the eternal Givingness to fulfill the need...the spiritual understanding that fulfillment is the natural process of the universe,
that the answer forever precedes the question. Such a consciousness, with all things added, is the right of Sonship. Thus, per-
manently written on every heart was the realization of God and
the Father-Son Relationship. While this Reality would be buried again under the rubble of ignorance and misperception, it
could never be removed from humanity's consciousness.

The kingdom is within you now, and did not Jesus give the
instructions, the code words, to find the realm of At-One-
ment? Did he not say "Search by the narrow gate"? This means
to confine your thinking to spiritual truth and restrict your emotions to the love and goodness of God. It is to remove yourself
from "this world" and seek only the Holy Path within.

Jesus said that he came bearing a sword, not peace. Amicable
nonviolence among the spiritually asleep would have maintained the world in its state of insanity. A tranquilizing of mind
and emotions in a lower state of consciousness could well lead to
a race of vegetables in human form. The sword that Jesus
referred to is the cutting edge that must be applied to *personality* to remove all that is blocking *Spirituality*. The fathering consciousness of greed and selfishness plants its seeds in the
mothering emotions of man, giving birth to fear and distrust,
with corresponding actions on the physical plane. Jesus came to
set man against these "parents," for true peace can come to this
world only after human nature has been transcended and the
greater part of the mind-aggregate is spiritual.

Jesus did nothing in vain. Through the flame of his consciousness, which embodied the fullness of Truth, he touched
the hearts and minds of every soul, including all living on the
planet today. No one, visible or invisible, escaped the touch of
his divine energy. Hence, there is not an individual consciousness in all the universe that does not know, in its secret place of
Knowing, that man is one with God, that the Spirit of God
eternally lives within and as each individual being, that those
who call themselves humans are in truth Holy Ones from the
spiritual realm on a journey through the third dimensional
plane for the experience of it. Without this Knowledge, con-

cealed as it may be in the dream of ego, man would continue to walk in circles of darkness, lost in the Lie of the Sin.

Through the releasing of his very Essence, the most potent and form-changing energy to enter the earth plane up to that time, Jesus also activated a new, quickening vibration in the body of the planet. Earth slowly began "rising"—moving into a higher electromagnetic field with a dramatic acceleration taking place in this century, which shall be explained momentarily. This ascent, to eventually reach the dense etheric state, requires a corresponding change in the physical structure of all life-forms. The three lower kingdoms are adjusting to the frequency change through the evolutionary work of the devas. The human kingdom, however, has generally elected to work out its own salvation following a path of evolution based on the correcting of karmic patterns through experience. This is, you might say, the long way in reaching the spiritualization of consciousness—and this slower process is enabling Earth to evolve at a more rapid pace than most members of the human family. The effect felt in individual lives can best be described as mental-emotional-physical pressure and a fragmented consciousness, which the human experience is mirroring as worldwide tension, a break-down of principles, heightened hostility and intolerance, and a lowered resistance to disease.

Did not Jesus anticipate the laggards? Yes, most certainly. He also knew that Earth must be lifted up for the benefit of the entire planetary system. Remember that man was given the way and the means to move with the transformation, but the law of free will could not be transcended. Jesus activated the identity Atom in man, thus liberating the *Christos* indwelling. Those who accepted the truth of their divinity were, in essence, "saved." They were called Christians—not in the sense of a closed in religion—but as bearers of Light from within. Today those Lights of the World can be found in every religion, and it is the spiritual oneness of the Lights that is *repeating* the energizing process in the Twentieth Century that Jesus initiated two thousand years ago. The Light Beings, in physical and non-physical form, are continuing to serve in the transformation of individual consciousness so that those who *choose* may advance with the planetary ascension. They are, as a group, working as the Mind of Christ.

Jesus removed the seal and released the energy of Oneness of Creator and created. And now another seal has been broken with the releasing of the energy of the atom. The concept of matter disappeared in mind and all-that-is appeared in mind as pure energy. The finite became infinite, the outer and inner became one with a simultaneous inrushing and outpouring of the sacred fire. Man and Earth had entered a New Age.

Since that time, spiritual energy as cosmic rays has been focused on the field of humanity's consciousness to prepare it for what is now called World Healing Day. This preparation is in the form of a gentle radiation to soften hearts and open minds. Any further intensity would so substantially affect thought-forms that wide spread chaos would prevail. The next step must be taken by the people of Earth. With sufficient Light emanating at that precise moment (noon Greenwich time, December 31, 1986), a dramatic shift in consciousness will take place. As the radiation continues, a new Love Vibration will be the instrument to modify behavior, change attitudes, and dissolve the destructive patterns buried deeply in the collective consciousness. The effect, in time, will be peace...not a humanly-defined peace, but a Christ-Ordained Peace.

Jesus has indeed been the vital link in this quest for a peaceful planet, and he may well be considered the Master Wayshower and Savior of the world.

◇ ◇ ◇

A question about religious intolerance.

Many of the western Fundamentalists of today are the very ones who cruelly persecuted the Christians during the two centuries following the crucifixion. Thus, a working out of karma. For the most part, however, they are ones who have a soul commitment to the worship of a God-Man. It is a form of mind control to bring forth the religious experience through service to personality in imaged form. The words "mind control" are used to define this practice, as the object of devotion becomes a reference in mind for the purpose of controlled thinking. Do not condemn this practice for it is one of the many ways of salvation—if bigotry toward another's faith is not developed along the path.

Fundamentalists may condemn the New Age because the spiritual teaching appears to be abstract, abstruse—which is completely contrary to their chosen path of surrendering to an actual person as Lord. This disapproval will fade, as will the harsh judgement by those of a mystical leaning toward a Fundamentalist's worship of a personality.

The balance is coming. The Golden Age is dawning. It will be a profoundly simple way of life compared to modern society...an age of kindness, respect, tolerance, goodwill, trust, love. Love and simplicity will be the cornerstones of the New World. The time is approaching.

◇ ◇ ◇

Question about reincarnation.

You have reported that reincarnation is a fact. True, but it originated as a man-fact, not a God-Fact. Reincarnation was not a part of the Cosmic System—not a law or principle of the Plan of Creation. As man expressed in form and his consciousness of *body* expanded, the intensity of the awareness grew so strong that it became essentially hypnotic. So powerful was the focus that the form side of life became the principal means of self-identification. Knowledge and consciousness of Essence was replaced with a perception of man-as-form.

Except for a few Souls who retained the knowledge of consciously altering vibratory rates to lift the form into the higher energy—and there continues to be such Souls on the planet today—mankind was now imprisoned on the Earth plane. The cessation of vital functions of the physical vehicle was the only release, the only door to the higher realm. Even though the life-span was many times the average of today, the gradual lowering of the vibratory activity eventually affected disintegration of the form and the Soul was liberated.

Once the earliest Souls were freed to return to the higher plane, there was an awareness that *the original perfection of man could only be regained in the vibration where the ideal state was lost — the energy of Earth.* Thus, the Spiritual Collective, man's own spiritual consciousness in oneness, established the Law of Rebirth. It is now a part of what you may call the Law of Evolution.

It was also deemed more advantageous for Souls to incarnate in groups, to participate in the search for the divine flame as a member of a group, each working together for the benefit of all. Have you not recognized a perfect stranger as a member of your group?

Do not become absorbed in reincarnation. One cannot move swiftly along the Path while looking backwards. Look for the Light in unselfish service to others, knowing that each step forward in this lifetime is one less step required in another.

There are many among you who are taking your final steps and shall return through rebirth only by your choice in sacrifice for those mired in the dream. Still others will master the lifting of the physical form, a transmuting of the gross energies or dense matter into a finer vibration body suitable for ascension. They will retain their body-patterns, thus escaping or transcending the Law of Rebirth — should return to physical form be necessary for world work.

⋄ ⋄ ⋄

3

The Lessons — Part II

Question regarding the Bible and literal interpretations.

To serious students of this sacred Work, it is obvious that the Bible, as it is now presented, does not reflect exactness, as in a mathematical principle. Taken passage by passage, contradictions abound. Yet, the historical symbology of the Old Testament is unparalleled, even though represented are but faint reproductions of the original writings — and the New Testament, with all its alterations, is a Manual of hidden Truth. The Divinity of Man is the quintessence of the Holy Book. . . it is the spirit of truth underlying all recorded principles. Still, man seeks lesser truth and accepts as reality a misinterpretation.

A person's truth is created from that which is believed, as accepted from all manner of exposures, teachings, and mental searchings. These beliefs, right or wrong, are then reinforced and personified as truth through religious study — accounting for such diversity in quotings of "absolute fact." Can not any position, true or false, be proved in the Bible?

An example. A person may believe in, and express as truth, blood sacrifices as a means of salvation. This began with the ritual slaughter of animals to appease the gods, and later became an element of the purification rites of Christianity with Jesus as the substitute through his sacrificial death. Today, millions believe the misconception that grace may be realized only through the blood of Jesus, authenticating the belief by quoting him as saying his blood is shed for the sins of man. Again, inaccurate translation. It was his *vital force* that he came to release into the world. In modern English the word would be *energy*. Through the radiation of his Christ Energy, which was incorporated or "eaten" by the mind-aggregate, man was given the means of retrieving his lost identity and freed from the darkness of ignorance.

Jesus did not write a word of the New Testament. The writings represent an accumulation of ideas, altered in the passage of time—in some cases to prove consistency, in others to conceal the high wisdom which otherwise would have been removed. In the sayings of Jesus as reported, there was much allegory, which even today is not widely understood.

The Bible must be read and studied with open mind and heart if the sacred teachings are to be found. Do this. First, however, study the evolution of the Bible, the sources of the New Testament, and examples of Bible symbolism. Then you will be ready to discover your truth, the highest of which is the message of God indwelling, God as man. Seek these passages in the New Testament, and write your story of the Truth of Divinity—the Truth of all.

Author's commentary: Following the above communication, I immediately began the process of research and writing according to the steps given. The result of this personal effort was a greater understanding of the Bible and the Truth of Being—much more so than if I had merely "heard" the information as words in consciousness. Sometimes The Teacher gives us homework to make a more substantial impression in our "body of convictions." Here is a brief summary of the completed assignment:

1. The Evolution of the Bible.

Regarding the Old Testament, "only late manuscripts survive, all (with the exception of the Dead Sea texts of Isaiah and Habakkuk and some fragments of other books) based on a standardized form of the text established many centuries after the books were written." (Harper Bible Study, Zondervan Bible Publishers)

In other traditional Bible References, we find that the Hebrew Bible was translated into the Greek language about 280-130 B.C. This Greek Bible, called the Septuagint, was the Bible of the early Christian Church until the conquest of Rome and until the Latin-speaking world required a translation in the Latin tongue. The early Latin translations were all made from the Septuagint.

The different Latin translations current in the second, third and fourth centuries led Jerome to translate the whole Bible (384-405 A.D.) from the original language into Latin. His translation (the Vulgate) *differed so much from the others* in general use that it met with great opposition. However, before many centuries, it became the Bible of the Latin-speaking world and was adopted as the official Bible of the Roman Catholic Church by the Council of Trent, April 8, 1546.

In the second century a translation was made from the Hebrew Old Testament into Syriac for the Christians of Northern Syria. This made three versions of the Bible for use in the early Christian Church—the Greek Septuagint, the Latin Vulgate, and the Syriac.

In the fourteenth century, Wycliffe (1320–1384) translated the first English Bible, not from the original Hebrew and Greek but from the Latin Vulgate, a translation of a translation. In 1526, Tyndale printed and distributed the New Testament in English, translated from the Greek.

Early in the reign of King James I (1603–25), he appointed a number of learned Bible scholars of England to produce a new and better translation of the Bible. After several years of careful work they produced, in 1611, the Authorized King James Version of the Bible, which the Harper Bible Study says is filled with errors: "The King James Version of the New Testament was based upon a Greek text that was marred by mistakes, containing the accumulated errors of fourteen centuries of manuscript copying."

In 1881, the King James Version of the New Testament was revised, followed by the Old Testament in 1885. The American

Revision Committee revised this work, and in 1901, issued the Bible known as the American Revised Version. In 1952, the Revised Standard Version of the Bible was published, which is an authorized revision of the American Standard Version published in 1901.

2. Sources of the New Testament.

According to The New Standard Reference Bible, "The books of the New Testament were written after the death of our Lord and before the close of the first century." In the Biblical Encyclopedia, the origin of these books can be traced as follows: "(1) In Paul's time there were *collections of sayings, which were repeated concerning the earthly life of Jesus.* One collection, known as Q (German quelle, 'Source') is important to us. (2) Mark, working upon a diary of Peter or upon some of his sermons preached at Rome, wrote his version of the Gospel. (3) Matthew and Luke, with Mark and Q before them, wrote their versions, *picking out what would be of interest to their readers or what suited them best.* (4) A disciple of an eye-witness (probably John) used the Gospels as his sources and gave us the Fourth Gospel." (Italics are mine)

3. Example of Bible Symbolism.

In the Condensed Bible Commentary, the question is asked, "Why did Jesus tell his disciples to buy swords?" The Commentary explains: "He spoke in figurative language, as he frequently did, and they, misunderstanding him, interpreted his words literally, supposing he alluded to present defense. Seeing that they misinterpreted his language about the swords, he closed the conversation with the words 'It is enough'."

The Commentary also states that "we do not know of any denomination but one which would insist that its members regard as inspired every paragraph of our present version of the Bible."

So what have we learned from this excerpt from the homework assignment? My impression is that the Bible is on a parallel track with the story of Man, i.e. Man was created perfect, descended into the karmic world of the third-dimensional plane, and by following the flicker of the Light within, began the search for the lost Identity through the Law of Evolution. Similarly, the Bible was originally written under Divine Inspiration to reveal the essential nature of man and provide a map for the journey home. But it, too, was transformed (altered) to mirror man's mortal ego—yet the truth of individual divinity remained within its pages to serve as a beacon of Light on the path. And through a corresponding evolutionary process, it is slowly being retranslated to reveal the lost "Identity" of its original essence. (Discoveries of ancient Bible manuscripts continue to be made, and I believe that before the close of this century, an ancient text predating all others will be unearthed in Egypt.)

And now to complete the final step in the assignment— "Seek these passages (of Truth) in the New Treatment, and write your story of the Truth of Divinity—the Truth of all."

4. A Story Depicting the Truth of Being.

Throughout the Bible are passages emphasizing the Oneness of God and individual being. I chose but a few to incorporate in this Message of Truth to myself—and to you.

You are the light of the world, as taught by your Elder Brother. Know this and the darkness will flee into the nothingness from which it came. Know your Self and the gates of consciousness will open to reveal the Truth of all who walk the Path of Discovery. The Truth is the Light within, the radiance of the Christ, the Reality of you. Express this Light that you are! You must *let your light so shine before men, that they may see your good works, and give glory to your Father who is in heaven.* | Matt. 5:14

Matt. 5:16

When you let Spirit express through you, what is seen is the Light at work, not the personality. The Light does not make mistakes or commit errors in judgement. The Light is Perfection. *You, therefore, must be perfect, as your heavenly Father is perfect.* While this may | Matt. 5:48

not seem possible under the constraints of ego,
Perfection is your natural state of being, for you
are the Father in expression, and the fullness of
God dwells within you.

It was the Master who said, *"Pray then like
this: Our Father..."* — thus identifying for all
time the truth of sonship. Each is a child of
God until the coming into spiritual maturity,
but even the child is of God for the Spirit of
God is the Essence out of which all things are
created. As the child grows into spiritual adult-
hood, the Power of the Inner Presence becomes
the only power in consciousness, and the commandment must then be followed to *heal the
sick, raise the dead, cleanse the lepers, cast out
demons.* Truly, *nothing will be impossible to
you.*

Yes, *all things are possible to him who
believes* in heart and mind, and millions now
walk Planet Earth with such a consciousness —
the Knowledge of the kingdom and its power
and glory. You possess the kingdom now, for it
is written that *the kingdom of God is in the
midst of you.* Know this and claim your sonship, your Christhood. Believe in Jesus' words
*"Is it not written in your law, I said, ye are
gods?"* Dare to express your Identity! You are
not a mere mortal, for *the Spirit of truth dwells
with you, in you. You yourself are full of goodness, filled with all knowledge,* for you *have
received, not the spirit of the world, but the
spirit which is from God.*

Know that God's Spirit dwells in you. Meditate on the Truth of your being...contemplate
the Presence within morning and night, day in
and day out, until you realize the Truth that *it
is no longer I who live, but Christ who lives in
me.* You are more than a human being, for all

Matt. 6:9

Matt. 10:8

Matt. 17:20

Mark 9:23

Luke 17:21

John 10:34

John 14:17
Rom. 15:14
1 Cor. 2:12

1 Cor. 3:16

Gal. 2:20

people are from above, *chosen before the foundation of the world...to be holy and blameless.*	Eph. 1:4
Commit yourself to God and only God, the *one God and Father of us all, who is above all, and through all, and in all.* Dedicate your life	Eph. 4:6
to *let this mind be in you, which was also in Christ Jesus.* Turn within now and feel the love	Phil. 2:5
of God, the love of *Christ in you, the hope of glory.* Understand with the fullness of your	Col. 1:27
being that *Christ is all, and in all.*	Col. 3:11
Never again accept the idea that you are less than divine. *Stir up your pure minds by way of remembrance* and let all thoughts of being a miserable sinner separated from God fall away.	2 Pet. 3:1
We know that he abides in us, by the Spirit	1 Jn. 3:24
which he has given us. Therefore, *you are of*	1 Jn. 4:4
God. *He who is in you is greater than he who is in the world!*	
Knowing this, what on earth is there to fear? God is the only Cause, the only Power, the only Presence, the only Life, so do not look to the outer world for your protection, your health, your supply. God's love provides everything,	
and *his love is perfected in us.*	1 Jn. 4:12
Be still and let the Christ within, your Holy Self, manifest as every good thing in life. Even now you hear the words...	
"Behold, I make all things new."	Rev. 21:5

Research the Bible and write your own message.

The Bible is truly a Codebook of hidden Wisdom and Truth. Ask your Higher Self, the Spirit of You, to reveal the Divine Inspiration contained in this Sacred Work, and write a Statement of Truth or a meditative treatment based on your new understanding. In addition to the scriptures noted in my message, you might also review the following verses:

31

Source	Key Words
Matthew 10:20	Your Father speaks in you.
Matthew 23:9	One is your Father.
John 1:9	The true Light.
John 14:12	Greater works.
John 17:5	The glory which I had with thee.
John 17:23	Perfect in one.
John 20:17	Your Father, your God.
Acts 17:28	In him we live.
Romans 8:16-17	We are children/heirs of God.
Romans 9:26	Sons of the living God.
Romans 10:12	Lord of all.
Romans 11:16	If the root is holy, so are the branches.
1 Corinthians 2:16	We have the mind of Christ.
2 Corinthians 6:16-18	I will live in them. ...you shall be my sons and daughters.
Galatians 3:20, 26-27	God is one...you all are sons of God...put on Christ.
Galatians 4:1,6	Owner of all the estate...you are sons.
Philippians 2:13	God at work in you.

Colossians 2:9-10	Fullness of the Godhead... complete in him.
2 Timothy 1:6-7	The gift of God within you...a Spirit of power.
Hebrews 10:16-17	Laws in hearts...remember sins no more.
James 1:17-18	Perfect gift from above...first fruits.
1 Peter 1:16	You shall be holy.
1 Peter 4:10	Each received the gift.
1 John 3:1-2	We are God's children.
1 John 4:6	We are of God.
1 John 4:13	We abide in man and he in us.
1 John 5:18-19	Any one born of God does not sin...we know that we are of God.
Revelation 3:20	I stand at the door and knock.

The *Metaphysical Bible Dictionary,* published by Unity School of Christianity, is an excellent resource book for interpreting the esoteric meanings of Scriptural names, and every serious Truth student should have a copy. For example, understanding the spiritual meaning of *Jesus* and *Christ* can be very helpful in your Bible studies. Here's a brief excerpt from the metaphysical definition:

> *"Jesus represents God's idea of man in expression; Christ is that idea in the absolute....The Christ is the man that God created, the perfect-idea man,*

*and is the real self of all men; Jesus Christ is this
Christ self brought forth into perfect expression and
manifestation."*

Let's conclude this chapter with a quote from *The Superbeings:* "The inspired, infallible Word of God is the Christ
indwelling each individual. The Bible was not intended to be
interpreted literally in all its parts. It must be read through the
heart and interpreted through the spirit."

4

The Science of
Co-Creation

Because of free will, we have the choice to accept or reject the boundless good that is ours. We are continually co-creating our life story according to the state of our consciousness. We provide the patterns for the Power, and what we experience is what we believe and accept as true.

In life, the daily events of fortune and misfortune occur as a result of the *trend* of our thinking and feeling. Every thought and emotion count for something. Each is a thread that is eventually woven into a thought-form, which must by law be expressed. Look at the majority of men and women living today on Planet Earth. Thoughts flow in and thoughts flow out — many being strong enough to strike an emotional chord — and the weaving of threads begins. The parent thought-forms, grouped as clusters of associated thoughts, deal primarily with self-identification, the purpose and meaning of life, God, the death experience, and life after death.

For example, a person thinks of himself as a human being. He exists visibly, therefore he identifies himself as a body, and his body consciousness transmits how he sees himself. He also identifies himself as a thinker — a personality — and through his mind he conceives his own self-image, which is a combination of his own thoughts about himself and how he feels others think of him.

Now we have a personality in physical form on the stage of life with a multitude of performers to help him experience his consciousness...mother, father, brothers, sisters, friends, antagonists, wife, children, employers, co-workers, ministers, and even strangers. With each interaction with the role players, more threads are woven, and in time the fabric of his life is a crazy quilt of thought-forms: happiness and sorrow, good and bad times, success and failure, health and sickness, life and death.

The purpose and meaning of life? His thought-forms say "don't expect too much...get others before they get you... plan for old age...hard times are inevitable...get all you can while you can"...etc. And so a lifestyle is created with the emphasis on security, learning to cope, and waiting for the temporary pleasures of the weekends.

What about God? The individual in our example may think of the Supreme Being as a vague, abstract Something, or an Old Man in heaven who takes glee in arranging a life of trial in payment for a sin committed by an unknown ancestor millions of years ago, or a God in the form of a Man who appeared on earth 2000 years ago whose teachings somehow led to a distorted interpretation that he was the *only* means of salvation. Whichever, the thought-form expresses itself as futility, doubt and skepticism — or fear, guilt and resignation — or intolerance, bigotry and hostility.

And death? "Earth to earth, ashes to ashes, dust to dust"... first illness, then pain, and finally the end of it all in darkness. Oh, the dread, the terror, the sorrow, the loss! The inevitable catastrophic crisis called death looms just over the next horizon — and all these thoughts throb as one in his consciousness.

Life after death? He considers it with unknowing, uncertainty and inconclusiveness. Or perhaps it's a hell if he's bad, heaven if he's good, and somewhere in between if he's in the gray area. And there's always the possibility that he will just sleep in the spiritual world until awakened by a savior, or be a part of a group that suddenly pops out of their graves when Jesus returns.

Now take all of the above thought-forms and belief systems,

blend them together and see what you have. You have the kind of insanity that race minds are made of, which is the mental-emotional base for most humans, i.e. birth and trauma, childhood and contention, adolescence and struggle, maturity and conflict, old age and resignation, death and fear, afterlife and bewilderment.

It doesn't have to be this way. Enlightened men and women have been working to change humanity's thinking for thousands of years, and slowly but surely the collective consciousness is turning toward the Light. One idea that is unlocking many doors is *Wholism*. Think of it this way: Rather than be condemned to a life that is incomplete, fractional and flawed, why not follow Jesus' instructions to *"Be ye therefore perfect"* and enjoy a life that is full, complete and total?

To move in that direction, you must begin to control your thinking and build thought-forms that will manifest as good-for-all, including yourself. In essence, I am talking about the development of a partnership with all the levels of your consciousness in order to co-create a new life, a new world, a new reality. To set the stage for the process that follows, ask yourself—which set of beliefs—A or B—will help you move with freedom and joy toward that circle of wholeness?

A	B
The Immanence of God (God Within) and the divinity of man are teachings inspired by the devil.	You are the Self-expression of God, and the Spirit of God dwells in you, as you. You and the Father are one.
All men are conceived in sin with a depraved nature and destined for damnation.	The idea of original sin is false. That a God of Love and infinite Wisdom would tempt man is absurd, and is not in keeping with the nature of God.
The perfectability of man is not scriptural and is therefore impossible.	As God individualized, man has an unlimited potential— even to the point of perfection.

Man cannot find true happiness on earth. Life was meant to be a struggle, and if you are truly enjoying life, you must be in league with Satan.	Gladness, joy and delight are the natural conditions of the soul. Jubilation is the Truth of your Spirit; exultation is the Reality of your being.
The unity of all life is a false and Lucifer-inspired doctrine.	Every visible thing is an expression of God...all is God in different degrees of manifestation.
God is vengeful, accusing, jealous and withholds your good unless you have been saved by the blood of the cross.	God is Love, and it is the Father's good pleasure to give you the Kingdom.
God cannot be reached except through an intermediary.	The Voice of God speaks directly to each individual.
Death is the final curtain of life and an entrance into the unknown...a time of fear and trepidation.	There is nothing to fear for there is no death — only the passing from one experience in consciousness to another — a birth into a new life of learning and growing in the Light.
Man can only be saved through Jesus' ransom for sin. Therefore, there is only *one* acceptable religion — all others are heathen / pagan cults whose followers are doomed forever to hell and eternal punishment.	Man was never doomed or damned. He is eternally a spiritual being, forever one with the Father within, and he is "saved" from the hell of this world through the realization of his true identity. And while there are many paths, there is but one Destination.

Would you not agree that thought-forms and belief systems based on the divinity of man, the love of God, the naturalness of happiness, the normal state of wholeness, the principle of abundance, the Allness of God, and the oneness of God and man are more in keeping with the Truth of Being than all the teachings to the contrary? I think you would, yet ideas based on sin, guilt, depravity, sickness, lack, separateness, vengeance, judgement, condemnation, hell and punishment are the predominate characteristics of the collective consciousness of mankind. No wonder the race mind is said to be insane!

If you are ready to come out from under the dark cloud and restore *your* world to sanity, let's go to work—concentrating on rounding out your circle of wholeness and moving above a consciousness of *need*. And since you are on the spiritual path as a serious Truth student, I'll assume that your mental-emotional patterns are basically sound and only a few adjustments are necessary. However, if you still have "unsound and unreasonable" ideas (traits of insanity) about God, death, and life continuing beyond the veil, seek understanding from your Higher Self and weave those holy thoughts into freeing, constructive and uplifting concepts using the process that follows.

Thought-Forms Based on the Truth of Being Can Change Your Life
Again, let's define a "thought-form." It is a cluster of associated thoughts on one particular point or issue which gathers energy and establishes a powerful vibration, causing an effect in the physical world.

Understand that the Christ of you, the Spirit of God within, is eternally expressing thought-forms based on the Highest Good for all. In constant radiation is the High Vision of joy, love, peace, wholeness, abundance and freedom. However, in order for this Energy of Fulfillment to reach the third-dimensional plane, it must flow through the rings of consciousness within your individualized energy field. If all the levels of consciousness are in alignment, the Force for Good finds an open channel for an effortless demonstration of "as above, so below." but if there is not agreement, or alignment, in consciousness, the God Energy is stepped down in vibration to be of one accord with *your* dominant thought-forms to honor the principle of free will. We have the choice of cooperating or resisting...we can accept or reject our good.

Thought-forms are initiated through the moment-by-moment thinking of your conscious mind. Threads of thought are fed into the subconscious and the building process begins, with each related thought coming together by the law of attraction to form distinct energy patterns. These are the Patterns of Life through which the Christ Energy flows to manifest corresponding physical equivalents. What you believe becomes the reality of your life.

Once the subconscious believes in a particular thought-form, that idea may become rather fixed and unyielding. And when you attempt to change it, there may be a strong resistance. Why? Because you've constantly fed your subconscious with conflicting information, so it has taken the dominant *trend* of your thoughts and built a nice, neat belief system, and it doesn't want you tampering with it. Just think of all the "vignettes" you've played in your mind over the years. After a time your subconscious became so confused with your yo-yo game playing that it couldn't tell the difference between serious mental programming and the negative drift of your imagination. So it settled on those thoughts charged with emotion to build its "truth." Now the bottom line is this: If your subconscious does not agree with you, it will not cooperate with you. Without its cooperation, the particular vibration for the good you desire will not be established, and the Creative Energy will continue to flow through and express a less-than-positive thought-form in the visible world.

The way around this problem is to work with the subconscious in a teacher-pupil relationship to change its thinking and educate it with a higher truth. It's as if your subjective nature believes that the world is flat. Suggesting to it that such information is false, and that the earth is in truth round, may only result in an interior punch to the solar plexus as the subconscious registers its disfavor with your thinking. The same thing may happen if you tell it you're in radiant health, or abundantly supplied, or a magnet for a loving relationship — if the trend of your thinking over the years has built thought-forms saying just the opposite.

It is vitally important to know where there is disagreement, because the negative vibration will give you the opportunity to focus your teaching in one specific area at a time in a reeducation process. Try this exercise with me. Speak the following affirmations aloud, then silently, and monitor your feeling nature to see if there is even the slightest negative response.

- God's will for me is perfect health.
- The healing currents of the Christ Life are flowing through me now.
- I am healed, whole, and in perfect health.
- The activity of Divine Abundance is eternally operating in my life.
- God is prospering me now and abundance flows to me in streams of plenty.
- I was born to be rich!.
- Through the activity of Spirit, there is now a divine attraction for my perfect mate.
- The Love of God flows through me to express in all my relationships.
- My life is filled with warm, loving, joyous people.

Wherever you have a negative blip, you have a block — so your objective now is to eliminate the blocks and become a co-creator with Spirit. Let me give you a brief example based on a personal experience, and then we'll go through the co-creation process step-by-step.

A few years ago, the prompting from within suggested that Quartus develop a Center to share the practical application of spiritual principles. I immediately went to work to be an open channel for the manifestation of the land and the facilities. However, I noticed that whenever I used a visual meditation to "see" the Center fully operational, I experienced a negative buzz in my feeling nature. Later I was informed by my Higher Self that my subconscious was not in agreement with this project, and would therefore block the Creative Energy required for its manifestation. I was told to get into a very relaxed state, address my subconscious as "friend" and inquire as to the reason for the disagreement. I did this, and the answer that welled up into my conscious mind was that the subjective "I" did not want the responsibility for developing, building and maintaining such an activity center, further stating that it would be an invasion of privacy and that I would be burdened with the "busy-ness" required in such an endeavor when my primary desire was to write books. I realized then that I would have to change the thinking of that level of consciousness by convincing it of the benefits of such a Center, and I did this through the construction of a thought-form that it could accept and believe in. And once there was agreement and the levels of my consciousness were in proper alignment, the Quartus land was made available along with a purchase plan that could be implemented without a strain on the Foundation's financial situation at the time.

I realized later, however, that the new thought-form was not locked in with any degree of permanence. Within a few months after building a temporary office for Quartus and moving into the home already on the property, I let my vision drift downward and became anxious about getting everything accomplished according to *my* timetable. And it wasn't long before the old idea of resisting change reared its ugly head. We must deeply and securely *implant* the thought-forms and not just tap them in with a few repetitive affirmations, as you'll see in the section that follows.

Implanting New Thought-Forms in the Co-Creation Process

Go back to the list of affirmations and see where you experienced a negative reaction. Only health, abundance, and relationships were covered because our research shows that these three areas are the most sensitive, with the matter of supply being the number one priority for a majority of people. That's why I have chosen financial sufficiency to use as the example in discussing the creative process. If supply is not a problem for you, please continue reading so that you will understand the principles of thought-form building, which can be applied to any depressed area in your life.

The Pattern of Abundance. If you have been working on the Forty Day Prosperity Plan without success, the reason was lack of agreement on all levels of consciousness. Let's see what we can do about that.

Let's quickly summarize the process, and then we'll go through each step. You begin by putting your thought-form of abundance in writing, making certain that you are very clear on what you wish to bring forth and taking great care that each word, phrase and sentence evokes strong, positive and joyful feelings and mental images. Write and rewrite the statement until you are perfectly satisfied with it — then present it to your subconscious. Read it very slowly and "listen" for any negative response. If there seems to be resistance, pause and ask why. If the answer seems to be a repetition of old tapes, firmly but lovingly instruct your "pupil" on the principles of abundance, teaching with logic and clarity. Follow this procedure through the entire statement and keep at it until you have a total consent from your subjective nature. Once you do, the concurring vibration will accelerate and with your assistance, it will move up in your energy field to make contact with the Higher Frequency of Abundance emanating from the Christ Presence. At this point, there is an alignment of energies. . . a channel for the Divine Expression is open. . . and a pattern of your highest vision is the blueprint for the visible manifestation. Now let's look at the individual steps.

Shown below is an example of a thought-form for abundance. My words may not stimulate your emotions and images, so you may want to write your own statement. In any case, remember that the first step is to put the thought-form you wish to express *in writing.*

I am the Spirit of Infinite Plenty individualized.
I am boundless abundance in radiant expression.
What is expressed in love must be returned in full measure.
Therefore, wave after wave of visible money supply flows to me now.
I am a mighty money magnet and oceans of money engulf me.

I am wonderfully rich in consciousness.
I am bountifully supplied with money.
I now realize my plan for abundant living.
I see my bank account continually filled with an all-sufficiency to meet every need with a divine surplus.
I lovingly see myself sharing this bounty for the good of all according to the Father's guidance.
I happily see every bill paid now.
I joyfully see every obligation met now.
With great delight, I see the continuing flow of this money used with love and wisdom as I create the perfect scenes according to my highest vision.

Now create the complete scenario in your mind of exactly how you will use this continuing supply of money, particularly during the next 12 months. In your imagination, use as many of your senses as possible to create a vibrant, dynamic, ecstatic motion picture of *you* enjoying the fullness of your abundance. Work out every detail until you are completely satisfied with the picture.

The next step is to present the thought-form to your subconscious, pausing after each line to see where the blocks are. Here's a hypothetical dialog that should give you greater understanding of this phase of the process.

You: **I am the Spirit of Infinite Plenty individualized.**
Sub: "That sounds like a pretty materialistic way to describe God."
You: **Not at all. The Spirit of God within cannot conceive of lack, limitation or insufficiency, and since abundance is Its true nature, Spirit's Law of Supply must be one of total and continuous All-Sufficiency. There is only Infinite Plenty in the Mind of God, and my mind is an extension of that Divine Mind, therefore, I AM the individual expression of that Universal Allness. In short, I AM Abundance!**
Sub: "I'll go along with that."
You: **I am boundless abundance in radiant expression.**

Sub: "I don't see you expressing much abundance in *your* life."

You: The Higher Self is the Expresser, the Giver of every good gift, the Supplier of all that is. Understand that the Christ within knows only unlimited, boundless, endless, eternal abundance. This Knowingness of Infinite Abundance is forever in perfect expression through *radiation!* The Energy of Supply radiates, flows through my consciousness, which includes you, my friend. If you believe that there's just enough to get by, then that's what will manifest because you produce the patterns for the Light. If you believe in a lie, which obviously you have up to this point, then the visible expression will be a misrepresentation of the Truth of Being. Look now and see the Omnipotent Energy, the Light, radiating from the Christ Center within, flowing out in all directions, literally covering the planet on which we live. *That* is the boundless abundance in radiant expression!

Sub: "I get the point."

You: What is expressed in love must be returned in full measure.

Sub: "What do you mean by that?"

You: That which goes out in invisible form as creative energy always returns as visible form and experience.

Sub: "Agreed."

You: Therefore, wave after wave of visible money supply flows to me now.

Sub: "Hold on. You mentioned the word 'money.' I don't have a good feeling about money because of all the negative thoughts and words you've expressed concerning your financial situation. Also, money has been called filthy and evil, and it's not considered very spiritual to want it."

You: My friend, money is currently the medium of exchange in this world, so if you don't want to be a burden on society you'd better change your mind on that subject. It's true that money is not supply, but it is most certainly the *symbol* of supply. It's also true that the love and pursuit of money just for the possession of it frequently results in dishonesty, crime, oppression, manipulation, miserliness, and unjust exploitation. But, my friend, money is also an indication of man's goodwill and God's Love in Action. An all-sufficiency of money can bring peace of mind and a measure of freedom to live more fully with ease and grace. And through the right and wise use of money, new and better services can be provided for the good of all. Also understand that the Energy of Abundance seeks to express in visible form for the joy of it! Substance-Light loves to appear and become that which is needed in the phenomenal world. Therefore, the principle of all-sufficiency, including money, is good, very good.

Sub: "Put that way, I have a lighter, happier feeling about money."

You: I am a mighty money magnet and oceans of money engulf me.

Sub: "Let's don't go overboard here. For one thing, too much money means too many responsibilities and too much time devoted to money management, and I'm not really into that."

You: Do not forget, my friend, that we are dedicated to the spiritual way of life, and while we will not limit the Unlimited, Spirit will not manifest such an extravagance that it would be a burden. The Holy High Self would never over-compensate by making us *servants* of money. By saying that I am a magnet for oceans of money, I am simply acknowledging the Law of Attraction and its awesome power to draw to me an all-sufficiency to meet my needs and implement my plans. And for this purpose, I am joyfully willing to accept all the responsibilities involved. Therefore, I am in agreement with Spirit's Activity of Abundance—and I decree that you also agree, that you now choose to participate in the co-creation process, and that you will now be a working partner in the manifestation of abundance!

Sub: "I am ready and willing to do my part."

In most cases you will feel the vibration of agreement for the

The Science of Co-Creation

whole thought-form before you finish the statement—*if* you have done your part to teach, instruct and educate with love and logic.

Once you have approval from your subconscious, the next step is to work *daily* with your statement and images. You begin by taking the preliminary steps that you would when going into meditation. Get comfortable, sit up straight, surround yourself with the White Light and take several deep breaths. Then focus your attention on your point of contact with the Spirit of God within and begin to love your God-Self with all the feeling you can arouse in your emotional nature. Once that vibration is established, redirect your focus to the area of your solar plexus. Now read your thought-form and follow with the period of creative imaging. Do this *three times* in each daily session, using the same words and mental pictures each time. Repeat the process daily until you are completely satisfied with the results.

Hopefully, I've emphasized the importance of building constructive thought-forms, but this activity should not be the main event of your spiritual life. Remember that your ultimate goal is to attain the Christ consciousness, so while you are building mind models as a step toward achieving wholeness, you should not neglect your contemplative meditation. If you are dedicated to realizing the Presence, you will have the Experience—and with the Experience comes a flooding of the Divine Thought-Forms into the subconscious. These are the Patterns of Living Truth from the Christ, and your role as a co-creator will simply be to maintain an open channel for the Christ Expression.

The primary thrust of this writing has been the *implanting* of new concepts in consciousness. In the chapter that follows is a story that deals with the *cancelling* of negative thought-forms—those that seem to be "cast in concrete"—and how they can be eliminated through unconditional love and forgiveness. It's the story of Tom, Dick and Harry, which appeared in the September 1986 Quartus Report.

5

Love the Boomerang
to Pieces

Somewhere, sometimes, each one of us amasses enough hostile energy in consciousness to release a silent but highly explosive force that functions just like a boomerang. And frequently we are not aware that the violent discharge has taken place because the pressure builds up gradually over a period of time and is released on a level beyond our sensory apparatus. In fact, as the malevolent thought-form moves past the final ring of consciousness, we may even feel a sense of relief followed by a stroke of "good fortune" in our lives. But on the astral plane the thought-form is streaking toward its culminating point and will one day make the return voyage to its maker.

Just like a homing pigeon, the thought-form (which I'll call "Old T.F."), will someday come home to roost. In truth, this dark energy will return to us to be transmuted, and if it's not, it will continue to come back into our lives at the most unexpected time. This energy is eternal and cannot be destroyed, so it seeks to be changed back into its original state of unadulterated pureness. That's our job, and no one else can assume the responsibility for us. Let me give you a few examples to make my point — in the story of Tom, Dick and Harry.

Tom had a tendency for years toward a particular form of illness, but through the practice of metaphysical exercises he moved above the vibration of the malady. A temporary healing, however, does not guarantee a spiritual consciousness, and one day Tom found himself caught in a web of greed and a resulting compromise of integrity. With the emotional warfare going on within him, Tom soon had the perfect recipe for a destructive thought-form: one part resentment, two parts guilt, mixed with equal portions of anger and deceit, stirred and poured over steaming envy. And it wasn't long before the hot energy attacked the most vulnerable part of Tom's physical system.

While in the sickbed Tom had time to dwell on his misdeeds, and the guilt, self-doubt and recriminations flooded his consciousness. That's all Old T. F. needed to be propelled out like a guided missile. The "release" brought waves of tears and seemingly much cleansing, and Tom's consciousness moved up a notch. Soon he was back on the job, and with a rededication to principles, found new happiness on the road to success.

But the business with Old T. F. was not finished. Like a boomerang it came back around. Just when everything seemed so rosy it struck again at that most vulnerable point in Tom's physical system. By now Tom had identified himself to family and friends as a "Truth Student"—one who has control over mind and body. Flat on his back in the hospital, he was *embarrassed!* How could this happen, he asked himself, and the whole self-recrimination process was repeated until sufficient pressure was built up to send Old T. F. back out into orbit... only to return again.

Now let's look in on Dick, who created his destructive thoughtform out of a weakness in the area of financial supply. That is his point of vulnerability—a karmic tendency you might say. So when Dick fell into a financial hole and had to face a money problem, those old energies of futility, fear, self-doubt, resentment, and condemnation started to pour in and the pressure began building. Before too long he was spending his nights on his knees and his days on the phone, talking first to God and then his creditors—praying for help in both instances.

Both showed mercy, and in time he worked himself back up to a level of sufficiency, which for some reason made Dick feel even more resentful toward those who didn't help him in his hour of need. That did it. Old T. F. now had enough fuel for a mighty launch, and off it went. Dick was driving home from the office at the time of the release, and suddenly he felt wonderful. The tenseness dropped from his shoulders and a feeling of forgiveness toward everyone on his hit list flooded his heart. He was ready to get on with the business of living.

With his new attitude, Dick began to enjoy a measure of prosperity and soon felt a sense of security. But Old T. F. had rounded the bend and was zeroing in on the target. Suddenly, or so it seemed, Dick's sales dropped, customers were past due in paying their bills, and there was insufficient cash-flow to meet the higher overhead (he expanded his business during the boom). Uh oh. Mr. Fear just walked into the pit of Dick's stomach, followed by all those delinquent relatives — futility, anger, resentment, et all.

"Why me, Lord? I've been damned good!" Now the wrath of Dick was upon God and Old T. F.'s fuse was lit. In time, Dick found solid ground again, but not before Old T. F. was rocketed back into astraland. Will Dick change before Old T. F. returns? Stay tuned.

And now we come to Harry. Harry walked through the dark night of the soul in his younger years, followed by two marriages that didn't work out and rejection by certain family members, all of which took its toll in terms of consciousness depression. You could say that Harry's point of vulnerability was relationships, and in his trial and error search for the "right" woman and a loving companion, there were many disappointments — each leading to a greater sense of rejection, a feeling of loss, and a hypersensitiveness to criticism. As this misdirected energy began to take hold in consciousness, a thoughtform developed based on the idea of rebellion and a sense of separation — a feeling of being disconnected from everything and everyone Harry thought was "good" in life. Perhaps unconsciously, he began to suspect people — and the pressure started building. Seeing others enjoying life while he was filled with despair soon ejected Old T. F. out with a silent blast.

For a time things seemed to clear up, but Old T. F. had other plans for Harry. Destructive thought-forms like to magnify an individual's point of vulnerability, and in Harry's case, that point was disconnection, dissociation, separation — the antithesis of relationship. But since Harry was already playing his part in the disconnect process, Old T. F. simply insured a more visible manifestation of separation. And what better way than through an accident, which would remove Harry from his work and the daily activities of his life.

Because Harry was on the spiritual path and working with consciousness, the first fall down the stairs resulted in only a few bruises. But the destructive thought-form wasn't transmuted. It only rested a spell, gathered strength, and went out again — this time to return as an automobile accident when a drunk driver "just happened" to swerve on to Harry's side of the road. Result: no serious injuries but a totaled car. Less than a year later, Harry fell again, ending up in the hospital this time with a fractured leg.

But Harry was far enough along with his spiritual studies by now to know that the cause of those accidents had to be within him. He had read the chapter on the Power of Love in *The Planetary Commission* and had listened to cassette tapes on unconditional love, so there was an awareness in his mind of this awesome Force. He remembered that all things could be changed by the Power of Love, that a negative situation could be loved right out of existence, that misqualified energy could be transmuted through love — so Harry went to work.

He began to pour all the love he could muster in his heart into the present situation. . .the circumstances surrounding the accident, the broken leg, his stay in the hospital. Then he went back in mind as far as he could remember, and with an open heart and purpose of mind, began to love and forgive his childhood, his parents, all of his so-called unhappy experiences, the failed marriages, the estrangements from family and friends, all the other accidents. He radiated love into every negative situation, condition, circumstance, experience and emotion. For hour after hour, day after day, Harry radiated the Energy of Love. Harry loved so much that he became Love in expression.

It's been over a year since Harry's last accident. And during that period he found and married a lovely and loving woman, a gentle soul who sees Harry as "the most loving man I've ever known"—a warm, caring, trusting, assured man who now treasures the oneness of his universal family.

Old T. F.? Well, he died somewhere out on the astral plane and was resurrected as one of Harry's many thought-forms of love.

What about Dick? Interesting case, Dick. After his last fall-on-his-face financial experience, he began to work seriously with spiritual principles and to meditate regularly. It was during one of his meditations that he "heard" a voice ask, "Why do you feel your life serves no useful purpose? Can't you understand that everything you do, regardless of how insignificant, is of *universal* importance?"

Dick was startled. He opened his eyes but that didn't prevent the memory-images from rolling through his mind. He *had* felt insignificant and of only minor importance in the divine scheme of things. He had even reached the point where social activities and relationships with friends seemed so empty, and the "have-to" responsibilities around the house were deemed so meaningless. He had just become a cog in some giant universal wheel, and his expectations of an abundant and fulfilling life had faded from his mind. He remembered a statement he used so often, usually when he was alone—"Oh, what's the use!" And it suddenly dawned on him that he was living a life filled with futility.

Within a month after this realization, Jan and I were in Dick's city, and he came to our workshop—arriving late but in time to hear Jan's talk about having a love affair with yourself. "I really haven't loved myself very much," he said later. But by the end of the day he began to see himself in a new light.

Shortly after we returned to Austin there was a letter from Dick, discussing his feelings about living an unimportant and ineffectual life and asking for ideas to change his consciousness. Here's part of my reply:

"The Universe does not compensate individuals based on the activity of work, but on the activity of consciousness. Accordingly, if you feel your life is empty and useless—that your work is insignificant—and that the things that are yours to do are really meaningless, then you will be pressing out of universal

Substance an income directly related to that consciousness: insignificant, trivial, useless and valueless. On the other hand, once you see yourself as you are in truth, and embody that vision in your feeling nature, you will move above lack and limitation.

"You are an heir to all that the Father has, all you have to do to receive your inheritance is to die to your old ways of thinking. Rising in place will be the Truth of you. . . a strong, vibrant, useful, significant, valuable, worthwhile, meaningful, loving, and fulfilled individual.

"The first thing I suggest is that you begin right now to love those empty places in your life FULL. Get to really know yourself and love that rediscovered you with everything you've got. Then look at every detail of your home and work life and let the love flow. Pour great love into every activity, whether mowing the grass, washing the car, fixing an appliance, talking to a customer, taking inventory, balancing the books, whatever! Nothing is too insignificant for the Energy of Love, so be a radiating Center of Love wherever you are.

"And, I'd like to see you spend at least fifteen minutes each morning and evening on the enclosed meditation."

The Meditation
I came into this world with a very specific purpose.
I came to fulfill a mission.
I came to love life and realize the truth about me.
I came to contribute to the salvation of this world.

I am a part of God and the fullness of the Godhead dwells in me.
In the Mind of God, no one, or no thing, is useless or meaningless.
Everyone and everything is of critical importance to the balance and
   order of the universe.
Without me, God would not be complete.
Without me, the universe would lose its equilibrium.

All that is before me to do, I do with happy enthusiasm.
For nothing is too insignificant.
And never again will there be a sense of futility in my life.

I am overflowing with gratitude to the Father for the opportunity to be in physical form at this time.
I am so thankful to be right where I am, right now, serving all who come my way with love, joy, understanding and forgiveness.

Recognizing my true worth, I now go forth with uplifted vision.
I see with the inner eye the loving and prospering activity of the Christ within.
I see with my physical eyes lavish abundance everywhere.
I am peaceful, powerful and poised, for I know who I am.

The end of Dick's story? There is no end, for life is eternal—but in the phenomenal world, Dick is now living a spiritual life surrounded by beauty and tranquility, and the karmic tendency of financial insufficiency has been transmuted.

And Tom? Well, Tom still hasn't learned to "love the boomerang to pieces." He continues to shop for a better doctor while working with spiritual principles when he has time. He's got one foot in the third dimension and trying to put the other one in the Fourth, and Old T. F. is heading home. You can almost hear Tom after he finally makes his transition...

"If I had only loved just a little bit more..."

6

Building a Foundation
for Truth

What is our objective in all of this spiritual work? What's the real reason for the School, discovering The Teacher, and meditating on the Lessons received from the Christ within? Why do we seek to train the subconscious and align our levels of consciousness? Why is so much emphasis placed on *Love?*

You know the answers. It is all part of a process of rising above the "human" sense of being so that we may realize the Presence of God and let that Realized Consciousness express Itself in our world. In moving toward this goal we may find a great deal of litter on the path in the form of self-imposed obstacles—and we must eliminate these barriers through intelligent reasoning, discernment, and understanding. In other words, we *think through* the obstructions to form a foundation for our truth. Let's do that now by applying some sound reasoning to our interpretations of letting go and letting God, human consciousness, and the meaning of reality. Then we'll add more firmness to the foundation by discussing the first law of the universe and the basic principle of life.

Surrendering to God

Remember that Spirit always expresses through us according to the tone, pitch and shape of our consciousness. If we "let go and let God" while maintaining a negative consciousness, the positive results will be minimal. As I pointed out on Page 29 in *The Manifestation Process,* "there are two ways of 'letting go and letting God'. One is to turn everything over to God while maintaining the same state of consciousness that produced the problem in the first place. This is like saying, 'Prosper me, heal me, but You've got to work around me and do it without my help'. Well, it doesn't work that way. But it does work when you let go and let God through your uplifted thinking and feeling natures. It does work when you surrender to the Father within after you have done your part in raising consciousness."

So we see that the first requirement for being an open channel is to lift the vibration of your consciousness to be of one accord with Spirit, i.e. "my consciousness *of* God *as* my health *is* my health. . .my consciousness *of* God *as* my abundant supply *is* abundant supply." We do not try to manifest health and wealth. Rather, we work spiritually to attain a consciousness of God *as* our health and wealth, and our consciousness expresses itself in the physical world.

It all comes back to seeking the Kingdom first—the consciousness of Spirit as the ALL-IN-ALL, everything invisible and visible—and then watching as all good things are added.

Human and Spiritual Consciousness

What is the difference? Perhaps the following chart will explain it for you:

Human Consciousness	Spiritual Consciousness
Accidents and safety	Safety
Anger and goodwill	Goodwill
Attachments and detachment	Detachment
Conflicts and harmony	Harmony
Danger and protection	Protection
Deception and honesty	Honesty
Despair and happiness	Happiness
Destruction and construction	Construction
Disease and wholeness	Wholeness
Evil and good	Good

Fear and faith	Faith
Greed and generosity	Generosity
Hate and love	Love — Unconditional
Insufficiency and sufficiency	All-sufficiency
Judgement and non-judgement	Non-judgement
Selfishness and unselfishness	Unselfishness
Sorrow and joy	Joy
Unforgiveness and forgiveness	Forgiveness
War and peace	Peace
Weakness and strength	Strength

And many more characteristics could be added to each list.

Now don't be thrown back into a sense of hopelessness just because you may identify your self as a totally *human* being. In Truth, we are all *spiritual* beings right now, and we are also "human" from the standpoint of the origin of that word. "Human" is related to Latin *homo* (man), and the root meaning of *homo* is "earthling." The human race is a Race of Earthlings. . . gods who took on low vibration energy and physical form for the experience of it. And in the process of the experience, we developed certain characteristics based on the idea of *self-preservation*. Accordingly, what we seek to change are those ideas. We do not want to promote a better human life using the old concepts related to self-preservation. So from this vantage point we ask: Why work or treat spiritually for a better body, bank account, or relationship with the same ideas in consciousness that produced the deterioration, the insufficiency, and the conflict in the first place?

This does not mean that we do not want to create a better life, or that we should not have the wonders, joys and things of this world. As spiritual beings in earthly forms we can have, be, or do anything! But humans filled with the flaws listed on the left side of the chart are going to have a tough time finding peace, fulfillment and prosperity on a sustained basis. We simply cannot have a better human life with any kind of consistency because of the duality of human consciousness and the attraction toward polarity, i.e. rich and poor, well and sick, etc.

In order to achieve mastery over the outer conditions, the

individual must first understand that there is a Higher Presence within Who is the Source and Cause of all that is good in life. There must also be a strong desire to escape from third-dimensional living, and a firm commitment made with the Higher Self to do so. This understanding, desire and commitment are followed by a period of seeking only the Realization Experience, which we discuss in the next chapter. Remember again that Spirit always expresses *through* us according to the vibration of our consciousness. Once we are in alignment and seeking only the Oneness of the Christ Presence, we can truly surrender and "let God be God."

The Meaning of Reality

Many metaphysicians condemn the material world as having absolutely no reality, being nothing but an illusion. If we are going to co-create a Heaven on Earth, we had better get beyond this absurdity, otherwise we are faced with the monumental task of reprogramming the subconscious with a totally illogical concept. If your objective consciousness finds it difficult to accept the unreality of that which is seen, heard, tasted, smelled, and touched, just think how the subjective mind reacts.

I raise this point because it represents a stumbling block for a great many Truth students. For example, if the physical body is simply an illusion, why work spiritually for a better mirage? If matter has no reality, then God-the-only-Reality certainly cannot manifest as something unreal, such as money. You can see the mind-trap we are setting with this kind of reasoning—particularly on the subjective level.

Understand that maya (illusion) was never a part of the Divine Plan. It was a theory conceived by a few sages of the ancient past to enable their followers to escape from the world by denying it. Their premise: You are living with poverty, squalor, and disease, but that's okay because that is your lot in life and all the world is a cosmic illusion anyway—so to want anything is wrong. Desire nothing and just be content to endure all those figments of your imagination and soon you will be absorbed into God where you can rest easy.

The tragic error of this teaching was in the identification of the visible world as unreal, rather than the false images in the consciousness of the individuals. The unreality was in the mental deception, the error thoughts based on ignorance that were fed into the subjective phase of mind, which maintained the wretched standard of living.

Here is an example that should help you grasp the significance of this. Think of a Master Architect who has the perfect design for a home. The blueprint (pattern) is absolutely true, pure, flawless, and correct in every detail. Now imagine that someone who knows very little about homebuilding took those plans and began construction. The end result? A stairway that goes nowhere, defective plumbing, deficient power, inferior workmanship, unfinished rooms, and an unsightly exterior appearance.

Now, where was the illusion? Was it not in the mind of the workman? Did not false and mistaken ideas and misconceptions go into the construction of the home? The home itself could certainly appear "unreal" to the Architect based on the original design, yet the house does have a measure of reality because of the very fact that it does exist!

The point I am trying to make is that the material world is indeed substantial, but what we are seeing are our misconceptions objectified. As our consciousness becomes more in tune with the Master Architect within, our world begins to reflect a more perfect pattern.

My truth concerning the material and spiritual world is that the Earth and the fullness thereof *IS*. Every visible thing is an expression of God. The four kingdoms exist as a present reality, and I am here to experience the delightful joys of each one. And if something seems to go haywire in my personal world (which is my consciousness made visible), I know that I have somehow blocked the Light—and it is my right and responsibility to clear the channel as quickly as possible. I don't dwell on error thoughts, mortal mind, mental causes, the illusion of the malady, or the idea that physical matter is not spiritual. Rather, I understand that the levels of my consciousness are out of alignment based on the *trend* of my thinking. As I adjust my consciousness, my world responds accordingly.

In *Practical Spirituality* I wrote about the healing and harming effects of consciousness:

> "...light is *energy* producing hundreds of trillions of vibrations per second in the form of light waves. Consider now that the Source of Light is within you and that light waves are eternally emanating from your consciousness, radiating as *lines of force*. These lines of force govern electrons (the electrical charges whirlings around the nucleus of atoms) and cause atoms to cluster in an energy field as a thought-form. This energy configuration is then 'stepped down' through levels of substance to become visible on the physical plane. Everything considered 'matter'—whether visible or invisible is made up of atoms, or pure energy. Therefore, everything seen and unseen is energy in motion, and this *energy of everything* is controlled by thought. The consciousness of the individual is the transmitter of energy and the directing force that destroys or creates form and experience.

> "The lines of force radiate from centers of High Vibration or low vibration, depending on the frequency of consciousness. You are either healing or harming...there is no in between. You can see now why the purity of thought based on the at-one-ment principle is of vital importance."

My purpose in repeating the above is two-fold:
1. Energy is Real. Matter is Energy. Therefore, Matter is Real.
2. Visible matter can be dematerialized, materialized, and changed—along with the experiences accompanying the manifest conditions—as you move up in consciousness to a High Vibration Frequency.

You have the Power of God to arrange you life and affairs to correspond to your highest vision, and you do not have to "put up" with anything less than perfection *unless you choose to!*

The First Law of the Universe: Divine Order

Divine Order is a Power concentrated right now in your individualized energy field, and in its awakened state it is vibrating, pulsating, radiating as the sun. When you experience Divine Order, your life is in balance, with a distinct feeling of equilibrium and symmetry. There is a sense of rhythm, as being in a natural flow. There is harmony as you find yourself filled with peace, contentment, and a unity with all life.

When your mind and heart are in agreement with the energy and power of Divine Order, you experience great joy, beauty in your surroundings, abundance to meet all your needs, wholeness in the body, and a realization of freedom to be yourself. No wonder that Divine Order has been called the first Law of the Universe!

In our experience we have found that one of the most powerful methods in dissolving the illusion of chaos and revealing the reality of order is through short, powerful decrees spoken audibly with a sense of rhythm and followed by a period of controlled visualization — all with a feeling of joy. For example:

I AM a radiating center of total peace.
I AM the harmony that will never cease.

I AM the power to do, to have, to be.
I AM the life that is eternally free.

I AM the way, the truth, the light.
I AM an eagle in preparation for flight.

(Pause a moment to feel the power building in your consciousness, then say:)

In the name and through the power of the Presence I AM,
I now decree Divine Order in my life and affairs.
Let the abundance I AM be revealed.
Let the wholeness I AM be manifest.
Let the love I AM be expressed.
Let the Will of God be done!

Now in the silence *see* the results of your decree. See in your mind's eye every detail and activity of your life as filled with peace, harmony, love, contentment, security, freedom, wholeness, beauty, abundance and joy. Get the feel of it, the thrill of it, the ecstasy of it. Laugh, sing, shout or cry tears of joy if you feel like it. Split the straitjacket, untie the ropes, remove the chains and stand up for God...the God-Self you are in Truth!

Living the Life of Divine Order.

Here are a few tips that may at first sound a bit strange, but they are designed to help you stay in the flow of Divine Order.

1. Be conscious of how you sit in a chair—aware of how you position your legs, arms and hands. Be poised, assured, with an air of self-confidence.

2. Be conscious of the way you walk. Move gracefully, relaxed—yet as the presence of power. Hold your shoulders back, be upright. Let your arms move naturally with your body.

3. Be conscious of your conversations with others. Be totally composed. Think before you speak, and speak with presence of mind. Let each word be harmless and harmonious. Listen with total attentiveness.

4. Be conscious of your thoughts. Think precisely. Bring the focus of your mind into each thought—and let each thought-form flowing out of your energy field be clothed only in love, peace, and the activity of God.

5. Be conscious of your emotions. Stop developing and rehearsing scenarios that cause fear, anger, resentment, and feelings of loss. Take total command of your emotional system. If a down vibration occurs, speak to the feeling with authority. Be detached, regardless of what is going on around you. Above all, practice unconditional love.

6. Be conscious of the activity of your work, whatever it may be. Be a witness to yourself performing each task with ease and assurance. See yourself in control of every situation. Be aware that everything you do is for the purpose of serving your Holy Self.

7. Be conscious of your surroundings—be alert, alive! Move into a new heightened awareness of the sky, the trees, the

flowers, the grass, the rocks, the Earth itself. Ponder nature. Contemplate the infinite Life Force in everything. *Be! Be* right where you are. Think deeply about your *Beingness.*

8. Be conscious of the Spirit of you, the Spirit-Self...the God-Life, God-Substance, God-Energy, God-Power, God-Mind, God-Intelligence you are in Truth. Begin to live now as the poised, powerful, peaceful, strong, self-confident, self-controlled, courageous, courteous, contented Being you are. You are God being you! *Watch* God being you. *Feel* God being you. *Know* God being you.

The Basic Principle of Life: Consciousness

Early in my spiritual journey I became aware that every problem I encountered was simply an outpicturing of my consciousness. Accordingly, I began to study the make-up of consciousness and meditate on its meaning—and over a period of time a new understanding of this principle of life was developed. Here are a few realizations along the way:

- It is *my* consciousness, and not the consciousness of others, that shapes my life and molds my world.
- Every single experience in my life, whether "good" or "bad", is created out of the vibration of my consciousness. The higher the vibration, the greater the degree of Good in my life.
- If I continually think about the possibility of being attacked by some form of disease, then I am developing a consciousness of disease, which must outpicture itself as a breakdown of the body.
- I do not work to develop a healthier body. Rather, I work to gain a consciousness of health, a spiritual consciousness of wholeness.
- If I dwell on limitation and insufficiency in *any* area of my life, I am building a consciousness of lack, and lack always attracts more lack.
- If I say "I can't afford" something, I am building a "can't afford" consciousness, and the law will bring more things and experiences into my life that I can't afford.

- In demonstrating an all-sufficiency in my life, I seek the realization that my consciousness of God *as* my supply *is* my supply.

- If I worry about what others are saying and doing, I am giving my energy to a so-called "outside power" — which emphasizes the belief in duality and keeps me anchored in the third dimension.

- I cannot judge the actions of others because they cannot help doing what they are doing. They are simply operating out of their present sense of identity, a particular level of consciousness.

- If I am uptight, heavy, concerned or anxious about anyone, I am becoming negatively attached to that person, which gives him/her power over me. I cut the cord on anyone who makes me feel less than I am in truth.

- When I expect anything from anyone, I am setting myself up to be let down. But when my expectations are directed towards Spirit, I am never disappointed. I place my faith in God and only God.

- Every person in my life is there by right of consciousness. Whether they are constructive or destructive, they are in my life through the Law of Attraction.

- If I look outside for my good, I am deserting my Source and closing the channel (my consciousness) to the flow of blessings.

- When I think of myself as not in my true place, consciousness will make sure that I am not. But when I realize that Spirit is never out of place, and I am that Spirit, the true place that always was is revealed.

Emmet Fox summed it up beautifully in his booklet, "Life is Consciousness." He wrote: "The explanation of all your problems, the explanation of your difficulties, and the explanation of your triumphs in life boil down to this: Life is a state of consciousness. That is the beginning and the end. That is the final step in metaphysics. All the other steps but lead up to that.

"Your so-called physical body is the embodiment of a part of your consciousness. The kind of work you are doing — whether you are in work that you love, or whether you are doing drudgery that you hate—is the expression of your consciousness at that point. The kind of people that you meet, the people that you attract into your life, are the expression of your consciousness about your fellow men."

And of course, the entire principle can be condensed into three words: *Like Attracts Like.*

7

Moving Beyond
Humanhood

To explain the necessity of moving beyond humanhood, let's
go back to your first awareness of spiritual principles, the dawning of Truth in your consciousness. At that moment sufficient
energy was released in your mind to enable you to overcome the
challenges and problems that were the most pressing in your
life. Your rediscovery of Truth was the result of a prompting
from your Inner Self to come up higher, and the impulse to
begin the spiritual journey was for one purpose only: to attain
the Christ Consciousness... to realize your divinity so that you
could then play your role in the divine scheme of things as a
world savior. But knowing that you could not, or would not,
devote your life to the total awakening to Christhood until your
mind could be relieved of the pressures of humanhood, you
were given that measure of spiritual energy to help you move
out of the pig pen and begin the journey home.

As you began to clean up your act, you got caught up in the
excitement and glamour of reconstructing your human world
and correcting the human picture. You forgot that you were
shown the spiritual path because your time had come — the fullness of time for you to embark on your spiritual journey. So you
began playing with the human scene, and in the process came
the understanding that the only limitations you have are those
you impose upon yourself, and your consciousness shifted into

the gear of unlimited possibilities. And through affirmations, spiritual treatments, creative visualization and meditation you felt stronger, healthier, more prosperous, and more loved and loving. As these positive thoughts and emotions cleared away some of the debris of false beliefs and negative energy, things began to happen in your world. The aches and pains slipped away, the needed money arrived at just the right time, and your relationship with people improved.

Most of us can identify with early success in our work with Principle. These demonstrations of the Truth were our faith builders, and they proved to us that consciousness is indeed the key to life — that as we change our consciousness, we change our world. Hooray for us. We found the yellow brick road and off we went, skipping merrily on our journey toward the mountain-top.

Then one day, an illness in the body, pocketbook or relationship flags our attention and we go to work to transmute it. But regardless of how hard we try, the situation seems to worsen, which releases the energy of fear to flood our consciousness. The spiritual path has been transformed into an icy slope, and as we lose our footing, we begin the downward slide on the seat of our pants.

What happened? The Presence has said, "Seek first *my* kingdom and everything that you could possibly need or desire will be added." But we decided to build our own human kingdom — and soon this emphasis on creating a better human life depleted the gift of energy, and then our "bloated nothingness" (as Emerson put it) got in the way of the divine circuits.

From experience I can tell you that humanhood can be improved only temporarily. . . that the ego can be inflated only so far before even the positive elements of consciousness (which are briefly outpictured as "relief") are overcome by the negative energy of human nature. How many times have we decreed "I am" such and such with the mind focused on the "eating, drinking, planting, counting man" (Emerson again) — the healthy and sick man, the young and old man, the rich and poor man, the successful and failing man, the good and bad man, i.e. the hu-man? Such mental/verbal action may boost the ego, but it also soaks up spiritual energy—and playing the human game is not dealing with reality. Only that which is spiritual is real... and lasting.

Understand that there is only one Spirit throughout infinity, and that is God. There is only one Substance—God; one Energy—God; one Self—God. But a hu-man is not God. Human nature at its best or at its worst, is the nature of the race mind—a collection of beliefs in duality and opposites, whereas in Spirit there is only ONENESS and ISNESS. God is not in human consciousness until God is realized—then it is no longer human. It is spiritual consciousness...it is Christ Consciousness.

Let's go back and look again at the early stages of our spiritual adventure. As the man or woman is indoctrinated to Truth principles, the awareness of the infinity of supply, wellness, etc. first dawns in the individual's lower nature, and through exercises in consciousness he soon believes (and continues to maintain the belief) that he of his own personality-self has all the God qualities. And as the ego establishes itself as the kingdom, power and glory, he begins to believe that through human efforts he can achieve lasting wealth, wholeness of body, and perfect harmony in his affairs. And so he concentrates on the *getting,* using "the power of God" to build a better *human* life.

We've all gone through the process. With each demonstration we begin to say that "I" have health, "I" have wealth, "I" have harmony, that "I" as a human being have these qualities of life, that "I" possess them. And the more the "me" senses it has, the more bloated it becomes. We can't see this happening because we're assuming (perhaps unconsciously) that the lower nature has all power, when in reality it is simply operating on that reserve of energy given to the mind. And when that energy is depleted, we are rocked back on our heels and our whole mental-emotional-physical system seems to go into bankruptcy.

This would not have happened, or at least it would have been much less severe—and we would have walked through the storm without fear—if we had gone on to be about the Father's business after that initial list of desires had been fulfilled.

But we didn't, and so in despair we go deeper into consciousness to find the answer. And one day we hear the instruction: "Seek the Realization. . . realize the Christ of your being and let all things be added." What does this mean? When you realize something, that something becomes *real* to you. When you realize the Spirit of God within you, Spirit becomes an actual Presence which your consciousness grasps as true and substantial—a present Reality. And then everything in your life changes to reflect the Truth of your being. The human scene becomes heavenly because it is no longer human. It is now the expression of God.

Realizations do not occur when we are trying to change the outer picture, however. They occur through contemplation of the Spirit within, through meditation on the contact and experience with the Presence, and through a receptivity to Spirit's Activity of Love. Through our devotion and dedication, our Holy Self becomes Real—and with each degree of realization, more fresh spiritual energy is released into consciousness.

As we continue on the Path with dedication to this kind of spiritual work, we find that initially we will have short, periodic realizations which release the energy in spurts—like a valve opening and closing. The spiritual energy that remains in consciousness following a realization is the healing, harmonizing, prospering power that produces what we think of as miracles.

Sometimes the energy of one particular realization is not sufficient to reveal the nothingness of a problem, so the "valve" must be opened several times, through meditation, to build an adequate reserve. But, and here's a word of caution, if the objective is to tune into Spirit and gather power for the solution to problems, the valve may seem to be stuck in closed position. To put it another way, going into meditation with the express purpose of handling a challenge will not bring you to the point of realization. You must leave your problems outside of the Secret Place and go in to meet your Maker solely for the Love Experience, the Holy Communion. That's when the Light penetrates the darkness of that which concerns you.

With practice, the Experience becomes a daily occurrence. And then a wonderful thing happens. During those moments of spiritual illumination, you perceive that you are not a human being after all. You see yourself as a spiritual being approaching the realm of Christhood.

What happens to the thinking mind while you are partaking of the Christ Energy during the Realization Experience? It moves into its rightful mode of awareness. It becomes the silent witness to the Activity of God...desiring nothing, possessing nothing, fearing nothing, resisting nothing...not trying to do, be or have anything. You are simply aware that you are a channel for the Activity of God.

A Personal Experience.

I had an unusual vision which gave me a deeper insight into this concept of awareness. I was shown a house, and was told that I was the house. My attention was then directed to a wall in the house. As I was staring at the wall a large hole appeared and I could see through to the outside. Then what seemed to be a large firehose was elevated to the position of the hole and water started pouring through. Watching the steady stream, I heard a part of me say, "I am a hole in the wall bearing witness to the flow. The water represents the Activity, the Word, the flow of Knowingness into manifestation of whatever is needed in my life. I cannot use or possess the water...I of myself can do nothing but be aware. The flow represents the All Good of the Universe, and yet, even while it pours through me, I cannot call myself good, rich, whole or perfect. To do so would call for the possibility of experiencing evil, lack, limitation and imperfection. That is polarity, and there are no opposites in the Mind of God. Therefore, I can only Be—and I die daily to the thought of having anything but the water, the Spirit of God—and the flow, the Activity of Spirit."

The words/thoughts stayed with me for quite some time, and as a result of that experience, I began practicing the idea of being "a hole in the wall"—an open channel for the outpouring of Spirit. I gave up all thought of trying to "have" anything or "be" anything as a human being. I did not seek abundance, health, harmony or the things of "this world." I gave up worrying about the form side of life and trying to do anything to change the outer scene. I totally surrendered to the Flow and

73

was content to let Spirit live my life for me.

Talk about a sense of peace! I can't describe the tremendous feeling when the cares of "my" world were removed from my shoulders. You see, if I was going to function less and less as a human being, then I had to give up (as much as I was consciously able to do) a sense of responsibility for conditions in the outer world. Otherwise I would remain forever on that roller coaster of highs and lows, rich and poor, healthy and sick, and so on. My only responsibility at that point was to be a channel for Spirit—to keep the channel open and witness the beautiful manifestations of Spirit.

During the process of being a witness, I found that I stopped using affirmations and spiritual treatments with the objective of conditioning consciousness along certain "human" lines. For example, why treat for prosperity when I'm no longer trying to improve an outer condition? Why affirm health when such action could also bring to mind the illusion of sickness. Instead, I took the attitude that abundance and health were really none of my business—those manifestations of wholeness and harmony were God's business, and I would simply relax and watch God being God through me. In essence, I neutralized my mind and emotions and let Spirit shift into the Drive Position.

There was a greater commitment to spiritual work then ever before during this period, but the emphasis was on being in tune with the Christ Vibration, affirming my Oneness with God, listening to the Word, opening myself to the flow-through of spiritual energy, and going about my day consciously aware of being a center through which the Divine Flow was taking place. I was very content just being a hole in the wall. But I did notice that the channel had to be kept open hour by hour, day by day, otherwise the mental delinquents of humanhood would try to come back in and take over.

After continuing the practice of being an open channel, something began to happen in consciousness. It was so subtle at first that I didn't catch the shift—and the beautiful and exciting thing was that it happened to Jan and me almost simultaneously. Again, it is difficult to put into words, but one day the Christ within became *real* to us. What was once an imaginary, idealistic, fanciful Something suddenly (to our consciousness) came forth as an authentic, certain, genuine Presence.

In my case, the "hole in the wall" identification dissolved and the "water flow" expanded to encompass my entire conscious energy field, enabling me to "see" a single entity of radiating light. The "thinking apparatus" (mind) of the physical plane man responded with a heightened awareness of, and feeling for, the Christ Self. This, to me, was the true meaning of attaining a spiritual consciousness.

Perhaps it would be nice at this point to say that we have arrived at Sainthood, but to do so would immediately result in giggles from the staff of The Quartus Foundation. No, it's quite obvious to anyone who knows us on a personal basis that we have not gone through the final crossing out of humanhood and the complete resurrection experience yet. There are many degrees of spiritual consciousness, and at our level Jan and I feel more like apprentices to the Master within.

Four Principles To Help You Move Toward The Realization Experience

1. *Love the Presence of God within you, your Spirit, with all your heart, with all your soul, with all your mind, and with all your strength.*

As I wrote in Chapter 11 of *The Planetary Commission* (and I encourage you to read that chapter again), "When you contemplate that Presence within, your very Spirit, with great love, that one-pointed love-focus will literally draw the awesome and incredible power of the universe right into your thinking mind and feeling nature. You take on the Power and you become the Power and you speak as the Power—and behold—all things are made new!"

Jesus called this the first and greatest of all the commandments because of the effect of this activity on consciousness, and if there ever was a "magic formula" for turning our personal worlds right-side-up, this is it! Meditating on your Presence with all the love you can feel in your entire being changes the vibration of your energy field and moves you to a higher frequency faster than anything I can think of. And in the process you are disconnected from the race consciousness, and false beliefs and error patterns are burned away by the fire of the Living Christ.

But this is not something you do once or twice a day. The secret is to *live* that Love of the Presence... to glance within many times a day and express your adoration... to court your Holy Self with total interest and attention.

Find your point of contact and begin the Love Affair this very day. That point may be the feeling of love in your heart, a Light seen with the inner eye, or perhaps an awareness in your mind of a higher Presence hovering in the background of your consciousness. Find that focal point — identify it as your connection with your Master Self — and pour all the love you can feel into it. Do it now.

2. *Recognizing that the Spirit of God within you is your Self, practice seeing your Self in others.*

Do this with everyone, particularly those who have been causing a negative blip in your consciousness. Try this: while you are focusing on your point of contact within and loving your Presence with the fullness of your being, gently bring to mind any individual who seems to be giving you trouble. Recognize that the Self you've been loving and adoring within you is the same Self of that individual. I've found it helpful to superimpose my point of contact over the image of the person, and then silently say, "I see my Self in you, therefore I can love you with all my heart and soul, for I am loving you as my Self." This simple exercise releases unforgiveness, resentment and condemnation in both parties and restores harmony to the relationship.

Remember, we are all One, so every negative thought you have about another person is really a destructive thought directed against your consciousness. You can certainly do great damage to your individualized energy field through judgement of others! Conversely, when you "salute the Christ" within another person, recognizing that his/her Spirit is *your* Spirit — and then radiating love to that Presence — the positive effect is felt in every form of life on the planet. And with each "salute" *you* are lifted into a higher vibration.

3. *God Knows!*

We are told in the Bible to "take no thought... your Father

knoweth that ye have need of these things. . .it is the Father's good pleasure to give you the kingdom." (Luke 12:22-32)

If you properly interpret these statements by Jesus in Luke, you will find a secret message that will give you peace beyond understanding. The key words are "your Father knoweth" because the Knowingness of God is the answer to the problem and the fulfillment of the need. Spirit cannot know something without taking action!

What Spirit is knowing, It is being, and since Spirit is Omniscient, It is eternally expressing (being) total fulfillment in every area of your life. Do you have a financial, health, relationship or job problem? You can be assured that Spirit knows about it, and that, my friend, is the answer to your prayer. Stop right here and think about your particular need at this point in time. Now say to yourself, "God Knows!" Yes, your Father knows that you have this need, but the Divine Answer-Solution-Fulfillment must flow from within out. The problem has already been solved in Mind, and now the solution must come forth into manifestation. But it won't come from somewhere "out there" *to* you. It can only come *from* you, through you!

Following a meditation period one day I was discussing a particular situation with Spirit, and I heard the inner Voice say, "I know. My part is done. The rest is up to you." That's when it hit me: the Knowingness of Spirit and the Activity of Spirit are one, therefore, the earthly illusion was already replaced by the Heavenly Vision, and my job was to *let* that Vision become manifest in my world. The instruction meant to stop taking thought (worrying) about the situation, and to become as clear as possible in consciousness for the radiation of the Light. My next step was to move out into the world to take any appropriate action under the guidance of Spirit.

4. *Recognize that the Activity of God is the only power at work in your life and affairs.*

Several years ago I picked up a little booklet written by J. Sig Paulson entitled "The Activity of God" — and in it were these words: "The Activity of God is the only power at work in my mind, heart, and life." This Truth completed the understanding that the Knowingness of Spirit and the Activity of Spirit are one!

I meditated on that statement for weeks and found that it worked wonders in helping me to clear my consciousness and let God be God. The Truth of the words helped me to understand that there was no power in effect—that the only cause, the only source, the only power, the only activity in my life was Spirit—the Knowingness of Spirit in action! With that realization, the fear of conditions vanished, and when the fear was removed, order was quickly restored.

Let's put the four principles to work now in a meditative treatment.

Spirit of the living god within, my Spirit, my very God-Self...my heart overflows with love for you. My Soul sings songs of boundless adoration for you...my mind reaches out to you in total devotion...and I radiate the love I am and have to you with all the power of my being. Oh, I love you so much! You are all I seek, and nothing in my life is more important than my oneness with you.

You are my beloved Self, and when I look within and feel and see and know you, I am beholding the Truth of all. Every person who has ever been a part of my consciousness is in Reality none other than you. I understand this, and now I can love everyone as my Self, for I see my Self in all, as all. My relationships of the past, present and future are now enfolded in love and harmonized for the good of all.

It is so wonderful to realize that there is but one Self, one Presence, one Power. Thank you, my glorious Spirit Self, for this understanding. And thank you for understanding me... for knowing every detail of my life...for seeing not only my needs, but also the fulfillment of those needs. God Knows! And because you know, the questions are already answered, the problems are already solved, for Divine Action eternally follows Diving Knowingness.

Now I can relax and behold the Activity of God, knowing

that it is the only Power at work in my life and affairs. The dynamic movement of Creative Energy is taking place now, in and through me. My Spirit knows exactly what to do, and is doing it now. The crooked places have been straightened, and that which concerns me has been perfected. The earthly illusion has been replaced with the Heavenly Vision, and I am now whole, strong and free.

8

Living
Your Highest Truth

Jan was in the kitchen preparing dinner one evening when she heard the inner Voice say, "I have something to say." She went immediately to her typewriter, and the next words were, "Please listen." A part of the transmission is as follows:

"Many think that by fighting the battle on the third dimensional plane they are making inroads. Not so. You cannot take the third dimension into the Fourth...you can, by lifting your vision, bring the Fourth Dimension into the third, however. And that is what you must do. Thought plus deeply felt emotion forms energy, and that which you place your energy into comes into manifestation—and is held until released through love, unconditional love.

"What you see with your mind and hold with your heart is the reality you experience. To change that reality you must change the picture formed by emotion and thought. Whatever is going on in your world you must look at, and if it is out of harmony, change the picture to one that fits. Then concentrate your energy on that picture and refuse to recognize the former.

"You must be in this world, but not of it, to bring about the change. Live here, be here, but do not accept that which is inharmonious to the Truth. Energy may be formed in any way thought and emotion directs, but that may be a miscreation. Only through purity of thought can the kingdom of Harmony come forth.

"Let thine eye be single. Do not be of duality—this comes from seeing third and fourth dimensionally simultaneously. Step across the line to Cause, true Cause, and the effect will be pure. Do not accept into consciousness that which you do not wish to see manifest. That which you think and feel will come forth. Only as you see clearly will the true picture of the plan emerge in all its glory."

In later meditation on these words, several ideas came to mind. First of all, when you take the offensive *against* anything, you are giving that thing power over you, and you are solidifying its position in your world. You will attract all of its negative characteristics into your life. So Jan and I ask you to determine where you're becoming emotionally involved with an inharmonious picture—and then to take action to "change the picture to one that fits." Through unconditional love and a vision of Reality behind the illusion, we can transmute the dark energy and restore each pocket of madness and irrationality to reason and sanity.

If we want Peace on Earth, the starting point is the man, the woman in the mirror. . . and the thought must be *harmlessness*. Do we just stick our heads in the sand and hope that all the evil of this world goes away? No, because that is another example of third dimensional activity. What we do is "bring the Fourth Dimension into the third", i.e. influence manifest thought-forms externalized on the physical plane by radiating spiritual consciousness through a vision of harmony, peace, and understanding. Let's never forget that we have the wisdom and power of the Universe in our hearts and minds, so let's begin to use those attributes to reshape our world and reduce to nothingness all that we have chosen to fear and fight.

I had a dream one night. The scene was a huge football stadium. On the field were thousands of men and women running around shooting at each other. From a seat in the stadium I witnessed this activity, and when I had had enough, I walked down to the field and moved among the shooters. I paused to speak to each one with such words as "Be in peace, my brother. . . you must love one another. . . go within and seek the light. . . we must all work in harmony and peace..." No one batted an eye and the shooting continued unabated. Finally, I walked to the top of the stadium, and in a voice that could be heard for miles, I issued a command using a four-letter word..."Drop the (bleeping) guns." Suddenly, the shooting stopped and every gun dropped to the ground.

I woke up thinking...well, when Self wants to get my attention there's no tip-toeing through the tulips. Obviously, trying to use tender reason with a frenzied crowd while remaining in third-dimensional consciousness (on the field) was futile, but when I went into a higher vibration (top of stadium) and issued a firm command that could be understood by the gun people, the appearance suddenly changed.

Who are the gun-toters? Ask yourself: Are you in emotional conflict with religious extremists? Are you, in consciousness, resisting the policies of any Government? Is your mind at war with Communism, Capitalism, liberals or conservatives? What kind of energy are you sending to the child abusers, the drug peddlers, the drunk drivers, and others who cause suffering on this planet?

Yes, you are witness to all these things because you are in this world to bring about the change! But are you doing your part? Are you living your highest Truth? What are you seeing? Can you see people of all religious persuasions finding *points of agreement* rather than areas of conflict? Can you see the militant Fundamentalists meeting New Agers in a spirit of unconditional love? Can you see every Government on the planet renouncing all selfish interests and actively seeking peace with every available resource? Can you see supporters of all social and economic doctrines willing to investigate, discover and adopt new systems based on peace, plenty and freedom for all? Can you see all the pockets of darkness in the world dissolved and replaced with right living, goodwill and harmony? If you're not seeing with purity of thought and emotion, you still have a gun in your hand and you are giving up your God-given Power of Transmutation.

So again I ask you to join me in dropping the guns, touching the Christ Vibration, and seeing this picture: The peoples of the world embracing in love, forgiveness and understanding...the mineral, plant and animal kingdoms all sounding their note of joy and freedom...the entire planet glowing with radiant Light.

Regarding prophets of gloom and doom.
All readings of the future are based on the present state of humanity's consciousness, *which can be changed!* Remember that *you* are a prophet of your own future based on your state of consciousness. The vision of Good that you "see" and believe as true will be manifest in your life—and—that which you fear will come upon you.

I am not saying that there won't be changes in this world. There certainly will be because the world cannot maintain its present course toward oblivion. And I believe that many of those changes for good will occur as a result of the global activity on December 31, 1986 *and continuing each month*. But it does take time for a "frozen lake to thaw"—and in the meantime we may witness upheavals in nature and instances of man's inhumanity to man—but the proximity to, and the effect upon, each one of us will correspond to the degree of our spiritual consciousness.

Now don't get momentarily hyper about where you are on a scale of 1 to 12. Just remember why you're in physical form at this time: To deepen your awareness of the Presence of God within, realize the Truth of your Being, and share the resulting illumination for the benefit of others. So we don't run around trying to be spiritual just to avoid problems. We work toward a spiritual consciousness because that's our reason for being, and if we find ourselves faced with a troublesome situation, we handle it based on where we are in consciousness at the time.

From this perspective, let's stop spending time worrying about the outer picture, conjuring up images covering all possible disastrous scenarios, and planning for a calamity. Let's concentrate more on growing into the Light, regaining our Oneness with the Presence of God within, listening to the inner guidance for any specific action we are to take, living according to the highest Truth we know, and continually projecting powerful thought-forms of the world safe and united in peace and unconditional love.

Let's steadfastly believe more in the Good, and let our understanding of the Truth of Being transform itself into a reality in our world. If we can do that, we will be doing our part in the co-creation process.

Learning to work with the inner alarm system.

While we do not focus on the outer picture with any anxiety, we do use common sense and spiritual principles in protecting ourselves from negative situations. And we do this by simply becoming invisible. Let me explain what I mean.

The energy of change that is coming in seems to be stirring up a lot of negative activity in many lives — and it's a part of the chemicalization process due to the awakening of consciousness. Also understand that the race mind is more vulnerable to the higher energies and is expressing agitation and resistance to the changes. The effect shows up in disturbances in nature, and in many "Phase One" minds that are closed, fixed, and unyielding. This brings forth a magnified projection of those individual's most dominant personality characteristics.

For example, the religious extremists will become more extreme, the fearful worriers will move toward hysteria, the futility-minded will use more drugs and alcohol, the lethargics will seem to be moving in quicksand, and the hostiles will be ready to fight anyone and everyone.

The energy of these people has the potential to create some sticky, unpleasant, and sometimes destructive situations if you happen to be on intersecting lines with it, resulting in hostile confrontations, accidents, equipment failures, and other disruptive situations. So the secret of avoiding negative action (from individuals *and* nature) is to make yourself invisible.

How? Understand that the energy of every potentially negative situation is of a low, heavy vibration. If you have been faithful in your spiritual work, living your highest Truth and spending time daily in meditation, your force field will be on a higher vibration than the energy wave on which the troublesome situation is riding, and you will be "above" the lines of convergence. However, many of us are not as dedicated to the Christ within and spiritual living as we should be, so at times we may find ourselves vulnerable to "the snare of the fowler." But even those below the halfway point on the journey have a helper on the third-dimensional plane. I am talking about that old friend, the subconscious phase of mind.

Through meditation, affirmations and spiritual treatments, the inner memory bank has been conditioned to harmony and order—particularly if it has been trained with love and logic. As a result, nothing can come to you now of a negative character without your subconscious nature picking up the situation miles away, or days or hours before it reaches you. When that level of mind knows something is going to happen that is destructive or disagreeable (where you need protection), it goes to work to attract your attention. You feel it in the pit of your stomach, or you have that queasy vibration in your solar plexus, or you feel a sense of danger. That's your subconscious alerting you that something unpleasant is coming. (I'm not talking about destructive boomerang thought-forms that *you* have created, as discussed in Chapter Four. I am referring to pockets of negative energy in nature and in certain individuals which may affect you through your unknowing affinity with that low vibration, which is usually brought about by stress, fatigue, and your being "out of sorts.")

To continue, let's say you're busy working, or driving the car, or fixing dinner, and suddenly, right in the middle of what you are doing you get that feeling that something's not right. The subconscious knows something is impending that the conscious mind doesn't know and it is getting ready to meet it. In essence, that "feeling" is your subconscious asking for your assistance in lifting the energy forces above the level that the negative situation is on.

If you will stop what you are doing and go to a quiet place where you can be alone, even if it's in a rest room, and raise your energy above the frequency of the impending menace, you will be immune to it. The negative situation or condition will not be able to find you because it will be coming in on a lower energy level, and when you rise to a higher level, you are no longer where you were and the negative activity "passes you by." You have literally become invisible to it.

Since the attracting vibration is usually emanating from one of the three lower energy centers, I have found it helpful to start with the root chakra and work up to the crown in a process of transmutation, using either meditation or affirmations depending on the time element and where I am when the "alarm" goes off. For example:

Focus on the appropriate chakra and meditate on, or audibly affirm, the corresponding ideas.

Root chakra at base of spine
In the Mind of God there is only Infinite Perfection, and everything in my life is an expression of that Supreme Wholeness. Nothing comes to me except from the Father. Only that which is pure, good and fulfilling can enter my world.

Spleen chakra below the navel
Divine Order reigns supreme in my life and affairs. All negative emotions are transmuted now, and I am joyous and free as I was created to be.

Solar Plexus chakra
The Light of God surrounds me and I am at perfect peace. I rest in the green pastures and beside the still waters in total serenity.

Heart chakra
Only the Activity of God is at work in my life, and God is Love. I let God's Love enfold me and care for me now.

Throat chakra
The Power of God is my eternal shield. I am totally protected by Omnipotence, now and forever.

Third Eye chakra between the brows
The Vision of God is my vision. I see only that which is right, good, and beautiful in my world.

Crown chakra
I am illumined in the Christ Consciousness. I know only perfection and harmony. I feel only peace and love. I see only right action and joyful living.

Continue the meditation or affirmations until you feel completely centered in the higher vibration...until you are invisible to "the noisome pestilence."

What is your Highest Truth?

What it is today, it may not be tommorrow, for we are evolving into a higher consciousness...moving ever closer to Christhood. Yet, we move from one level to another by living and practicing the highest Truth we consciously know on each level. When we realize one Truth, we are ready for the next step... and the process continues.

Your state of consciousness right at this moment is expressing all the Seeds of Truth that have been planted in your mind and heart, fed and watered through deep meditation, and harvested as Realizations. Thus, the fruit of your world is in direct proportion to the Truth that you have actualized. If the harvest has been meager, is it not time to plan for a more copious yield? To begin, I ask you to *use* the Truth that you already know. Just take "what you have in the house" this very day—that which you *know* that you know—and live it to the fullest of your ability. This using what you have with total devotion and commitment will accelerate the expansion of your consciousness and cause such a chain-reaction of realizations that you will literally fly to the Mountaintop.

What do you know that you know? You know that God *IS*— and that you exist as God in expression, therefore the fullness of the Godhead must dwell within the expression—otherwise you would not exist. You and the Father are one—and this One in consciousness is the Father of the seeking child, the Spirit of the Initiate, the I of the Adept. It is the Lord of Being, the Master Self within. It is God being *You*.

How do you practice, use, live this Knowingness? You lift up your vision and *see* only the Power of God at work in your world. You dedicate your life to the Omnipotent Christ within. You serve your Holy High Self with the fullness of your being.

Give your life to the Glory of God, and the Angelic Choir will sing songs of gladness heard throughout the universe as the Beings of Light joyfully exclaim..."Another One is coming home."

Even now they hear your words:

I listened for the eagle and I heard the call to commence the Journey Home. The instruction was so simple, yet the rewards so great: "They that wait upon the Lord shall renew their strength; they shall mount up with wings as eagles; they shall run, and not be weary; and they shall walk, and not faint."

I am now dedicating my life to the Living Christ within, and I am indeed strong. My youth is renewed like the eagle's, and I have risen from my sickbed and now stand forth with vigor and power, knowing only the Life Force of Wholeness. I am lifted above deprivation and scarcity and I am soaring in the limitless substance of abundance. I am protected under the shadow of the Almighty, and no evil can befall me. I am set on high, on a rock, above all sorrow and anguish. And my heart has been opened to love, a love so great, so unconditional, that it has attracted to me heaven's boundless measure of adoration.

I have given up the little self for the Holy Self and I have found the Way. I have wings as eagles, and into the heavens I have flown, a flight of joy and gladness that has taken me to the Secret Place on the Mountain, the very Kingdom of God. And here I run, and I am not weary; and I walk, and I do not faint.

The Dawn is here. The Eagles are flying.

APPENDIX

ANNUAL WORLD HEALING DAY

At noon Greenwich time, December 31, 1986, men, women and children around the world gathered to participate in the most comprehensive prayer activity in history a planetary affirmation of peace, love, forgiveness and understanding involving millions of people in a simultaneous global mind-link. The purpose: to reverse the polarity of the negative force field in the race mind, achieve a critical mass of spiritual consciousness, and usher in a new era of Peace on Earth.

It was called World Healing Day, the World Instant of Cooperation, World Peace Day a moment of Oneness to dissolve the sense of separation and return humankind to Godkind. Whatever the term or label, it was the New Beginning in restoring this world to sanity.

The majority of the individuals and organizations participating in this light of the World activity were operating under the umbrella of the Planetary Commission, a worldwide non-denominational, non-political organization without a headquarters, structure or staff. The Commission was and is simply a grass roots cooperative effort to unite people in a common bond of love and bring our planet back in balance.

The first formal announcement of the Commission was made on January 1, 1984, with the stated objective of having 500 million people on Earth consenting to a healing of the planet with no less than 50 million meditating at the same time. December 31, 1986 was designated as 169World Healing Day 170 and noon Greenwich was selected as the time for the healing meditation as it would encompass all time zones during that 24 hour period.

Word of this new Goodwill Task Force quickly spread, and when that 169moment in time 170 arrived on December 31, 1986, the Mind-Link represented all religious faiths on seven continents, in more than seventy countries, and in every state in the U.S. Over 500 spiritual and peace-oriented organizations around the world participated.

Celebrations were held in cities throughout North and South America, Europe, Asia, Africa, India, and Australia. In the Soviet Union thousands gathered in Moscow to 169think peace 170 and contemplate global cooperation.

In the U.S., a number of governors and mayors issued proclamations designating December 31st as World Peace Day, and gatherings involving thousands of people were held in areas and stadiums in major cities. Across America, other like-minded individuals came together in homes, churches, city parks, hotel ballrooms, in forests, and on mountains and beaches.

The Commission did not disband after December 31, 1986. In fact, it is expanding and gathering strength each year as greater awareness of the Event spreads around the world. Will you participate with us on December 31st of this year and the next and continue until the collective shift takes place? We ask that you join with other Light Bearers in your community, or if it is your preference, to be alone in coming into vibration with the Global Mind-Link to radiate your light, love and spiritual energy.

The World Healing Meditation that is being used by millions each year in the simultaneous bonding is shown on the following pages. Together we can usher in a New Beginning of Peace on Earth and Good Will toward all...as love flows forth from every heart, forgiveness reigns in every soul, and all hearts and mind are one in perfect understanding.

For more information on this Earth-changing Event, please write to the Planetary Commission for Global Healing, The Quartus Foundation, P. O. Box 1768, Boerne, Texas 78006-6768.

WORLD HEALING MEDITATION

In the beginning
In the beginning *God*.
In the beginning God created the heaven and the earth.
And God said Let there be light: and there was light.

Now is the time of the *new* beginning.
I am a co-creator with God, and it is a new Heaven
　　that comes,
as the Good Will of God is expressed on Earth through me.
It is the Kingdom of Light, Love, Peace and Understanding.
And I am doing my part to reveal its Reality.

I begin with me.
I am a living Soul and the Spirit of God dwells in me, as me.
I and the Father are one, and all that the Father has is mine.
In Truth, I am the Christ of God.

What is true of me is true of everyone,
for God is all and all is God.
I see only the Spirit of God in every Soul.
And to every man, woman and child on Earth I say:
I love you, for you are me. You are my Holy Self.

I now open my heart,
and let the pure essence of Unconditional Love pour out.
I see it as a Golden Light radiating from the center of
　　my being,
and I feel its Divine Vibration in and through me, above
　　and below me.

WITH WINGS AS EAGLES

I am one with the Light.
I am filled with the Light.
I am illumined by the Light.
I am the Light of the world.

With purpose of mind, I send forth the Light.
I let the radiance go before me to join the other Lights.
I know this is happening all over the world at this moment.
I see the merging Lights.
There is now one Light. We are the Light of the world.

The one Light of Love, Peace and Understanding is moving.
It flows across the face of the Earth,
touching and illuminating every soul in the shadow of
    the illusion.
And where there was darkness, there is now the Light
    of Reality.

And the Radiance grows, permeating, saturating every
    form of life.
There is only the vibration of one Perfect Life now.
All the kingdoms of the Earth respond,
and the Planet is alive with Light and Love.

There is total Oneness,
and in this Oneness we speak the Word.
Let the sense of separation be dissolved.
Let mankind be returned to Godkind.

Let peace come forth in every mind.
Let Love flow forth from every heart.
Let forgiveness reign in every soul.
Let understanding be the common bond.

And now from the Light of the world,
the One Presence and Power of the Universe responds.
The Activity of God is healing and harmonizing
    Planet Earth.
Omnipotence is made manifest.

I am seeing the salvation of the planet before my very eyes,
as all false beliefs and error patterns are dissolved.
The sense of separation is no more; the healing has
    taken place,
and the world is restored to sanity.

This is the beginning of Peace on Earth and Good Will
    toward all,
as Love flows forth from every heart,
forgiveness reigns in every soul,
and all hearts and minds are one in perfect understanding.

It is done. And it is so.

ABOUT THE AUTHOR

John Randolph Price is the co-founder, with his wife, Jan, of The Quartus Foundation, a spiritual research and communications organization formed in 1981. Prior to the founding of Quartus, John devoted more than 25 years to the advertising and public relations business, serving as executive vice president of a Chicago agency and president of a Houston-based firm.

He began researching the philosophic mysteries of Ancient Wisdom in the mid-1960s, and he has integrated those teachings with spiritual psychology and metaphysics in the writing of his many books. In 1994, he was presented the International New Thought Alliance's Joseph Murphy Award in recognition of the contribution that his books have made to positive living throughout the world.

For information about workshops conducted by John and Jan Price and their bimonthly publication, *The Quartus Report,* please contact The Quartus Foundation, P.O. Box 1768, Boerne, Texas 78006.

We hope you enjoyed this Hay House book.
If you would like to receive a free catalog featuring
additional Hay House books and products,
or if you would like information about the
Hay Foundation, please contact:

Hay House, Inc.
P.O. Box 5100
Carlsbad, CA 92018-5100

(800) 654-5126 • (800) 650-5115 (fax)

Please visit the Hay House Website at:
http://www.hayhouse.com